THE

STILL RISES

THE

STILL RISES

SURVIVING AND THRIVING AFTER GRIEF AND LOSS

SHAWN DOYLE, CSP

Sound Wisdom
P.O. Box 310
Shippensburg, PA 17257-0310

For more information on foreign distribution, call 717-530-2122.
Reach us on the Internet: www.soundwisdom.com.

ISBN 13 TP: 978-0-7684-0527-9
ISBN 13 Ebook: 978-0-7684-0528-6

For Worldwide Distribution, Printed in the U.S.A.
2 3 4 5 6 7 8 / 18 17 16 15

DEDICATION

THIS BOOK IS DEDICATED TO THE ANGELS OF MERCY— every doctor, nurse, counselor, psychologist, hospice worker, funeral director, psychiatrist, bereavement camp volunteer, friend, and anyone else helping those who are grieving the loss of a loved one. You never get the credit you deserve. You have angel's wings. Thank you all.

CONTENTS

CHAPTER 1

THE WORST NIGHT OF MY LIFE

"There is an hour, a minute—you will remember it forever—when you know instinctively on the basis of the most inconsequential evidence, that something is wrong. You don't know—can't know—that it is the first of a series of 'wrongful' events that will culminate in the utter devastation of your life as you have known it." —JOYCE CAROL OATES, *A Widow's Story*

I HAVE LIVED FOR 54 YEARS—AND I CAN TELL YOU THAT Friday, May 4, 2012 was without a doubt the worst day of my life. *The worst.*

You hear people say that all of the time. "I had the worst day ever," and, "Today was the worst day." I will never say that again because I have already had the worst day—and that day will forever live in my life calendar as the worst of all days— May 4, 2012. It started out a beautiful, pure, and innocent day. It was a Friday, and I have always loved Fridays because I love weekends. I was on a business trip and arrived home, landing in the early afternoon. I sent my wife, Cindy, a text message to let her know that I had landed and was on my way home from the airport. She jokingly texted me back, "CHKKK... CHKKKK—Oh OK. Rodger that—the Eagle has landed!" I texted her back wondering what the "chkkk" was. She said it was static on the radio but didn't know how to spell it. What a sense of humor. She was excited that I was home and said that she had missed me. I drove home looking forward to a nice, relaxing weekend.

I arrived at the house in the early afternoon and we had a very pleasant afternoon together talking, having a casual dinner at home, and just enjoying each other's company. I asked if she would like to watch a movie, and she said she didn't feel like it—she wasn't in a movie mood—but encouraged me to watch one myself. I opened up my Kindle Fire and found a movie that I wanted to see. I put on headphones so that I wouldn't disturb her with the sound. She was sitting on the couch surfing the Internet on her iPad, and I was sitting nearby in my easy chair. Even though we weren't talking, being in the same room was nice.

It's odd when I think about it. The night that your life changes, you never know in advance that it is going to be "the night" (maybe that is for the best). The night lulls you into thinking that everything is fine, that it is going to be a nice, happy, peaceful evening, and then suddenly the world tilts quickly to the dark side.

Around ten thirty at night my wife stood up suddenly with an alarmed look on her face. I looked up from my movie and instantly knew that something was very wrong. I mean, I had known her for 35 years, so I just knew. I took off my headphones and laid down the Kindle.

"Are you okay?" I asked, standing up.

"I don't feel very good," she said. Her body wobbled slightly side to side. She turned and ran quickly from the living room down the hallway toward the bedroom. I followed her because I was concerned she was going to fall over. She sat down in the bedroom on a wooden chair.

"I think you need to take me to the hospital." She looked a little sweaty. Her voice sounded a little off.

"Okay," I said.

I quickly put on my shoes, grabbed my wallet, cell phone, and my keys. I hurried back into the bedroom.

"How are you feeling?" I asked.

"I think you need to call an ambulance."

Now I was really alarmed. I stood right there keeping an eye on her as I called 911 on my cell phone and told them my wife was very sick and to send an ambulance immediately. "Please get here quickly!"

I disconnected the call and when I looked up, Cindy's right hand shook violently. Then she made a fist, tilted over, and suddenly fell onto the floor like a limp ragdoll. I was stunned and cried out, "Oh my god!" and called 911 back. "Oh my god, my god, my god! Get here now—she has collapsed!"

I was crying, sweating, yelling, and trying to revive her.

"Come on now…don't go…don't leave me, you hang in there! Come on now, come on…"

I was terrified. She was not breathing, her heart was not beating, and there was no pulse that I could find. There was no life in her, and if the soul is a bird—it had flown away up into the black night sky.

The paramedics arrived and I remember hearing them pounding on the door. I ran to let them in and the entire living room and hallway was awash with a dizzying watercolor of spinning blue and red lights shining through the windows, bouncing off the walls. I opened the door and told them to hurry, that she had collapsed in the bedroom.

A policeman led me into my living room so we could talk. I told him what had happened. The whole time we were talking I could hear them working on her down the hall. He told me I should call my daughter and have her meet us at the hospital. I called her and gave her a brief description of what was happening; she was in shock. After several minutes he went to check on how things were going. I couldn't take it anymore and had to walk outside to get some fresh air. It had started raining lightly, and it seemed somehow right that I was crying and the sky was crying at the same time. I was pacing in the yard and praying and saying, "Come on, you have to make it," over and over. After a few minutes the police officer asked me to come back inside, and had me sit on my entryway stairs in the hallway. He looked extremely grim, and by the look in his eyes I knew in my heart what he was going to say before he said it.

He then said the words I didn't want to hear. He cleared his throat awkwardly. "Well...Mr. Doyle...I don't know how to tell you this, but ever since the paramedics have arrived they have not gotten any response from your wife. They have been talking to the doctor at the hospital and reviewing all of the vital signs, and I regret to inform you that your wife has passed away." Those words froze in the air for about 15 seconds. I was speechless. He suggested I call my daughter back and have her come to the house and not the hospital. There have been a few times in my life when it felt as if I was a character in a movie and the movie wasn't real. The movie scenes were winding across the giant screen and I was in the reluctant lead role. That is exactly how I felt that dark, wet spring night.

In the blink of an eye, the sweep of a few turns on a clock, two flaps of a dove's wings, and my wife of 32 years was gone and became part of the ages. She was 50 years old, way too young and way too good to go so soon. Who could ever imagine it? How could anyone have ever predicted it? No one would or could. We always say things like "life is short," "seize the day," "appreciate what you have," and "make every minute count." They are handy platitudes which I think are easy to say, but I don't know if we always mean it. Do we really understand? We all take time with others for granted. I feel grateful that I was home with her and she did not suffer. It would have been awful for her to have died alone. No one ever wants to die alone.

It's hard to imagine, but that night got worse. Unfortunately, because she passed away at home, they couldn't transport her body. They had to call the medical examiner's office, which was the procedure in Pennsylvania that was followed in the event of a death at home. The policeman quietly explained he would call the medical examiner and would wait with me for the medical examiner's arrival. Two crews of paramedics came walking down the hallway with sad faces and their heads respectfully bowed. As each one walked past me in a funeral-like reception line, they reached out and shook my hand and told me they were sorry for my loss. Many had tears in their eyes. I truly felt bad for them; they had tried their best and despite their efforts, they lost.

I called my daughter and told her she shouldn't go to the hospital but to the house. I then called my friend Steven to tell him what was going on. Even though it was now 11:00 p.m., he came over right away. Within twenty minutes, I was sitting in the living room with my daughter, her husband, her husband's parents, and my friend as we waited for the arrival of the medical examiner. It was the longest night of my life, as we sat talking in hushed tones, trying to somehow forget that Cindy was lying in the other room, silent, her body still. It was a vigil without the candles.

The rest was a bad dream. The medical examiner arrived, sat me down at my dining room table, and interviewed me, wanting to know every detail of the afternoon and evening. I had to relive it by telling it. He then went into the bedroom, took pictures and measurements, and filled out a bunch of forms. At around two thirty in the morning, they asked if I wanted to tell her goodbye before they transported her body. I said that I would like to say goodbye, and gave her a last hug, and said a few words to her, even though I knew she was no longer there—it was just her body. It was a terrible goodbye. I told my daughter she could decide, but it would probably be best not to see her mom that way. They put Cindy on the stretcher, rolled her out of the house, and she left our home for the very last time. The policeman came over, put his hand on my shoulder, and said quietly, "I just wanted to let you know there isn't going to be an investigation." I hadn't thought about it for one minute and was a little shocked he brought it up. I had been a suspect for a while I guess. He did his job with dignity and empathy—he was a total professional.

Everyone was tired and emotionally exhausted. My daughter and her husband offered to spend the night with me, but I told them I would rather be alone. I don't know why I made that decision at the time, but I knew I needed to be alone. I saw them all out and thanked them all profusely for the kindness, love, and support. I told them that I would see them the next day.

I tossed and turned restlessly in bed that night and for the first time in a very long time felt completely and utterly alone. The house felt hollow and silent. I remember thinking over and over, "Where is she?" and even saying out loud a few times, "Where did you go?" That is the strangest part of all—how someone so vital, full of energy, and lively can disappear from the face of the earth. I knew where her body and her soul were— but where was she? The essence of a person seems impossible to extinguish, but somehow, someway, she was gone—the candle flame was out and would never be re-lit.

I slept very little that night, but the next morning when I woke up, the sun still came up. It has a way of doing that—the sun still rises no matter what. The TV was still playing and people were driving to work. People were eating breakfast and walking their dogs. The world was still spinning. I realized that it was real, that it had really happened. I had woken up with a label that I detested (a widower) and I was no longer married but single. All goals and dreams that we had as a couple were now canceled and were not to be. The quilt that was once our life had been taken apart overnight and was now just a collection of loose fabric squares with many missing pieces. It had gone from *our* life to *my* life. My heart was crushed.

The week that followed was a watery blur of meetings at the bank, funeral arrangements, visitors, flowers, food, urns, the coroner, a private family viewing, and the funeral. I will never forget the feeling of getting up that day and getting dressed knowing I was going to my wife's funeral, a funeral for *her*. It was a feeling I can never describe. Words whispered in tight hugs, people saying it was "God's will" and "God needed another angel" and "this too will pass" and "only the good die young." Saturday was huge, fragrant flower arrangements, soft hymns, tissues, and tears. I heard an amazing, powerful eulogy that captured my wife's essence, making people laugh and cry, filling many minds with wonderful memories of her and who she was. I was in the movie again. This time I was in the role of the bereaved husband and it was surreal. How did I get there? Why did this happen? Where was I? At my wife's funeral? Really?

I spent many nights wondering where Cindy had gone, as if she vanished in the night, lifted off into the spring breeze to fly across the meadows. I also battled my biggest enemies beyond grief—the lonely sound of an empty house and the terrible feeling of being totally alone. I would come back from a business trip, put the key in the door, and walk into a darkened house. I would walk in and say, "Hello, I am home!" I would then sheepishly realize there was no one to say hello to, and that was a soul-crushing feeling.

So now, reluctantly, I began a new life I did not choose. I had a life with Cindy, but now began my life after. I was part of a couple, now I was solo. I was married but now a widower—as categorized by society. None of this was my choice. The only choice I had was how I responded to it.

The "why" behind why someone dies so young and suddenly, is beyond my human comprehension, and I hope someday I will understand. I was told by some smart people to stop asking why. There is no answer. I had to rebuild a new life and yet always honor the old one. My team of brilliant advisors told me it would take time, but I would be OK.

WHY I DECIDED TO WRITE THIS BOOK

I simply wanted to share my story so that you can know my view, my perspective, and the basis for my perspective. This is the real story of what I lived.

I am not a doctor or psychologist or an expert in any way relating to death and grief. I am, however, a simple man who has experienced the grief of losing a wife and the grief of losing a child. So while there are many books out there written by psychological experts and grief researchers, I am not one of them. I do have loads of life experience to share and it is all real. I not only survived, but yes, I thrived.

I'm sorry, but I don't believe there are six magic steps or stages of grief. I don't believe there are any tips, tools, and techniques that work for everyone. There is no formula. Every person grieves differently, and I can't say what will work for you. I don't know if the things I did were "right," but they helped me heal and worked for me. I wrote this book for some very specific and heartfelt reasons:

I want to help.

I want to help people through the most painful, agonizing, soul-searching, and difficult times in their life and help them heal and move forward. As a professional speaker and author I have always specialized in motivation, with my personal and professional mission to make a positive difference in people's lives. If you asked me before this all happened, I honestly never thought that I would make a positive difference in a grieving life, but if I can help someone or lots of people who are hurting, I have then served my purpose. It's always a great feeling to give back to others.

I was told and encouraged to.

I know that one sounds a little odd but many friends, relatives, and associates strongly suggested that I write a book about grief—why? For some reason, they were impressed about how I handled my grief, how quickly I seemed to recover and heal. They also noticed how I took, at times, a very different and unique approach to grieving. I had not thought of writing a book about grief, but so many people told me I should, I decided there might be something to it. After discussing it with my family and others, and thinking about it for a while, I decided it was a good idea.

Experts are very wrong.

I have noticed that experts who speak and write about grief often speak about it from a standpoint of academic study or from research or interviews, but sometimes I think this is unfair because they have not experienced it personally. I have experienced it personally, and believe me, I wish I hadn't. I have lived it, and I will tell you what they got wrong.

Society is often wrong.

I see people in society giving advice to people grieving, but far too often they have no real practical basis for giving this advice. They don't know what they are talking about. They give horrible advice and say the wrong things. Maybe I'm a little bit of a rebel, but I decided to ignore many of society's customs as it relates to grief, and I did things a bit differently. So part of my mission in this book is to give someone who's grieving permission to handle grief in their own way and not worry about society's "rules."

Life is short.

If life is short (and I know it more than some people), then we should not be spending our time sitting in an empty room staring at the walls being sad. Please don't misunderstand what I'm saying—I'm not saying you should not grieve the loss of loved one. You always will. What I have learned is you should mourn, but life is too short to sit around for too long grieving. My goal in this book is to help a person suffering through a loss to shorten the amount of time of misery and unhappiness, so the person can move forward in a healthy way.

I want to give people hope.

My uncle, Scott Camp, who is a pastor in California, spoke with me by phone only a few weeks after my wife passed away. His advice was some of the best because it was infused with a message of hope. He told me that I was going to be OK, that I was going to have a new life, that everything would work out, and that I was strong. I needed to hear that, rather than the traditional doom and gloom. My hope is that this book can be a light of hope for you.

I want to shatter myths.

For some reason there is a lot of strange, bizarre, and often misplaced advice surrounding how people grieve and what people should or shouldn't do when grieving. I would like to shatter many of the myths to give grieving people comfort in knowing the truth about these misunderstandings. While you are grieving, these myths can be very disturbing and sound like they're true. I'm here to say that many things people say are not true, and in fact, are detrimental to the person who's grieving. So be very careful who and what you listen to.

WHY YOU ARE READING THIS BOOK

1. You have experienced a loss in your own life and have lost a spouse, a child, a parent, relative, or a close friend. You are trying to figure out how to get through it. If this is true for you—I am so very sorry. Having been through it, I bleed for you and I feel your pain. I am not saying that all grief is alike or that I know how you feel (I don't), but I do

know how hard it is. I want to extend to you and your family my sincere heartfelt sympathy and love. I want you to imagine that I'm reaching out right now, grabbing your hand and holding it to comfort you. It will be OK. I promise it will, and I can make that promise because I lived it. There is hope for the future.

2. You know someone who's experienced a tragic loss of a loved one and you want to help them. If that's the case, then you're a very special person. I commend you for wanting to help that someone go through a difficult time. Just know this—you may feel as if your help doesn't mean a lot, but I can tell you that the help, the love, and support that I got was incalculable in terms of value and how it helped me heal.

3. You are in a profession that deals with people who have had a loss—doctor, hospice worker, funeral director, etc. If it is you I am describing, I commend you for your work and wonder how you get through the door each morning with the angel wings on your back. Your work is truly remarkable. You are in my opinion an angel of mercy.

HOW THIS BOOK WILL HELP YOU

It is my sincere hope that there are several ways this book will help anyone who reads it:

Define myths and misinformation.

If you know what they are and you are ready to address them and think independently, you will be in a much better place. You will hear something and think, "Yeah—I was warned about this one." You can also decide if it is true for you or not. You can then smile and have a chuckle about it.

To know what you can expect.

If this is the first time you have been through the grieving process, it's nice to know what may or may not happen so that you are prepared. There will be many surprises both good and bad. There will be companies that won't know how to handle the death of your loved one, and even something as simple as removing a name from an account can be painful. I will share with you some of my experiences and how I decided to handle them, and you can decide for yourself how to handle them in your life.

Get assurances and hope.

I will give you some information and share with you real experiences in my life that I think you may find helpful, no matter where you may be in your grief journey. Half of the time, hope is just talking to someone else who has been through what you're going through and understands you. They successfully have gotten to the other side. It's like being on one side of a raging river and seeing another person standing on the bank across the way waving at you and saying, "Swim across—the water's fine!" Just knowing that someone else made it across the river gives you a feeling of optimism for the future.

Evaluate where you are.

I will help you think about where you are currently in your life, having just experienced a tragedy, and some of the things you need to start processing and thinking about in order to continue moving forward. Just because you are grieving doesn't mean that you stop living, and let's face it, there are lots of housekeeping things you have to do, like paying bills and maintaining cars and houses. There are still people depending on you.

Coping with grieving and healing.

I will be providing lots of tools, tips, and techniques for dealing with grief on an hourly, daily, and weekly basis. These are tools that I used. I will be sharing specific stories and examples of what I did to help my healing. Now in the interest of open disclosure, I will tell you that they may not all work for you, or they may not work at all. But I would urge you to give them a try, to see if they work even a little bit. In this case, even a little comfort goes a long way.

Thinking about society's rules.

I will be providing for you a list of the rules that society thinks you need to follow while grieving. I will also tell you how I reacted to these rules and how I handled people's reactions when I didn't follow them. Yes, it's true, there will be people who expect you to follow the rules, and when you don't they will not be happy with you. They have decided it is their job to tell you how to run your life, and by golly, they are right. Just ask them—they are experts (not).

Making sound decisions.

Unfortunately, almost instantly after a tragic death the people who are still around need to make a huge number of decisions and some very quickly. You will immediately be asked to make very tough ones. The night my wife died we had to decide in a family discussion if we wanted an autopsy. I was the one who had to make that hard decision only two hours after my wife had passed away, and let me tell you that was tough. I will give you some tools and techniques to help you think about what decisions you need to make and how to make them in your overall best interest.

Know about resources.

I will provide a list of helpful resources both online and real time that may help you in your journey of living with grief. Often it is not what we are experiencing in life, but the tools that we have available to us. Many times people just don't know where to find the resources they need. I have many resources—some of them conventional and some a little different.

Start planning.

I will review with you how to sit down and do some planning—short term, midterm, and long term. This will give you an opportunity to start thinking about and planning the future.

Taking care of yourself.

One of the biggest dangers of being in grief and dealing with loss is not taking care of yourself physically or emotionally. I'm going to give you some ideas about self-care and will encourage you to be extremely selfish during the time that you're grieving.

You have to take care of you, so that you can then take care of others. The stress of grief can be capably managed by using different self-care techniques.

Designing your new life.

I know if you are grieving that you probably don't want to think about the concept of having a new life. Unfortunately, life did not deal the cards in that way. So the idea is to play the cards that you are dealt, honor the loved ones who have passed, but start thinking about the road forward and about reinventing your life.

So I think this book can help in many ways.

What I can't do is take away what happened, and I can't restore your life to the way that it was before. It's hard. The thing that really stinks about it is we can't change it. Most things in our life we can say, "Well, next time I will do this differently." We get to do it over until we get it right. Death doesn't work that way, it is so permanent. What I can do is give you techniques, ideas, and thoughts that may help you in some way. This is a marathon, not a sprint—grief is a long-term process.

I come bearing good news. The good news is you can learn to live with it. Yes—the sun still rises. You will get better, the pain will lessen, and one day in the near future you will wake up and realize you are finally having a happy day or a happy hour or a happy minute. Life can be happy again—trust me. I know because I am very happy. I survived this experience, but more importantly, I am thriving in every area of my life.

To close this chapter I think Dean Koontz said it best about grief:

> Grief can destroy you—or focus you. You can decide a relationship was all for nothing if it had to end in death, and you alone. OR you can realize that every moment of it had more meaning than you dared to recognize at the time, so much meaning it scared you, so you just lived, just took for granted the love and laughter of each day, and didn't allow yourself to consider the sacredness of it. But when it's over and you're alone, you begin to see that it wasn't just a movie and a dinner together, not just watching sunsets together, not just scrubbing a floor or washing dishes together or worrying over a high electric bill. It was everything, it was the why of life, every event and precious moment of it. The answer to the mystery of existence is the love you shared sometimes so imperfectly, and when the loss wakes you to the deeper beauty of it, to the sanctity of it, you can't get off your knees for a long time, you're driven to your knees not by the weight of the loss but by gratitude for what preceded the loss. And the ache is always there, but one day not the emptiness, because to nurture the emptiness, to take solace in it, is to disrespect the gift of life.
>
> —Dean Koontz, *Odd Hours*

CHAPTER 2

MYTHS, MUDDLING, AND MISINFORMATION

*"In times of grief and great despair one must find
solace in the dawning of a new day."*
—SHANE PENDLEY

I DON'T KNOW WHERE OUR SOCIETY CAME UP WITH SO MANY myths and misinformation about death and dying, but it seems to me that many people have accepted myths and misinformation as *the truth* and they're not. They are myths, misinformation, fairy tales, propaganda, urban legends, and campfire tales. This is something to really be aware of—don't just take it at face value—what is the truth, and most importantly what is the truth for you?

I am very fortunate because I have been a professional speaker and trainer for the past 26 years. When I suddenly became a widower, I was able to apply everything that I have learned and taught for 26 years to my own life. I, in essence, became my own student. This gave me the confidence during a very difficult time in my life to be able to sort through what

I felt was the truth and what was not for me. So in this chapter I'd like to cover with you the myths and misinformation that areout there in our world and give you my thoughts and opinions to help you prepare for what you may experience as someone who's lost a loved one. Keep in mind that these are my opinions and what I found true for me.

MYTHS

Myth number one: "I know how you feel."

People will say to you that they "know how you feel," either because they think they do or because they have experienced loss sometime in their life as well. Let me clear that one up right away—*no one knows how you feel* because no one has lived your life. No one has experienced what you are experiencing right at this moment. Even though I am a widower, I can't honestly say that I know how you feel, and you can't honestly say you know how I feel. Everyone experiences grief differently. I have always tried to keep in mind that people who say things like that are people who have good intentions and are not trying to be mean or insensitive. Unfortunately, the person grieving can actually resent the person saying it because they're thinking, "There is no way on earth that person knows how I feel, because they have not experienced my loss." It can create anger and resentment.

My first reaction when someone says "I know how you feel" is that the person is arrogant in thinking they could possibly know how I feel. The reality is they are trying to make us feel better, they're trying to comfort us, and they're trying to take away our pain, so they just say whatever comes to their mind or repeat platitudes that they heard from others in the past. So the best approach when someone says "I know how you feel" is to ignore the words and pay attention to the intent—they're just trying to be helpful. Really. No one on earth knows how you feel. Once you admit that to yourself, it is a little bit liberating because you don't expect anyone to know how you feel because well, they just can't.

Myth number two: There is a certain way that someone should act when grieving.

This is the one that gets on my nerves the most. As a society we should define what grieving people should be doing and/or not doing. Really? The week after my wife passed away I was sitting at the house Monday through Friday, receiving phone calls from concerned friends and family, receiving visitors, and making funeral arrangements. It was the worst week of my life. It seemed as if the time between Friday night, when my wife passed away, and the following Saturday afternoon, when the funeral was held, lasted two long, painful, agonizing months. On Wednesday of that week, my daughter came over to visit and in her hand was the newest Muppet movie on DVD. I asked her what it was and why she had it. She said that all of us at the house were going to sit down sometime that day and watch the Muppet movie because things were too serious and too grim, and we needed to laugh a little. It wasn't a statement—it was a command. I smiled when she said that because I realized she was right. It was true.

We all sat and watched the Muppet movie, enjoyed it, and laughed, and it was a nice retreat from a week of hard grieving.

Yes, I'm sure that some people would be taken aback by the idea that Cindy's family was watching a Muppet movie five days after she died. They would say that it may have been "inappropriate" or "weird," but we really don't care what they say, or we shouldn't. Please don't miss this point—it is not up to other people to define how you act when you're grieving. It's up to you. Grieving is a very personal process, and because it's a very personal process, it's going to change depending on each person's personality, attitude, and experiences. So there is no one way to grieve at all, no right way or wrong way, no normal or abnormal way.

Two weeks after my wife passed away, I got a call from a business colleague who had heard about Cindy's death. After we had chatted for a while, she asked me where I was. I told her that I was at the mall shopping and she immediately responded with, "You are at the mall shopping?" I guess grieving people are not supposed to shop! After thinking about it for a few moments she then said, "Well, Shawn, I guess it kind of sounds like you. I mean, you always had a great attitude." It's almost as if there is a list—the list of things that grieving people are not supposed to do; anything outside of that list makes people a bit uncomfortable. Oh well. This is one time you don't need to worry about others—just yourself. Just be you.

Myth number three: There are stages of grief.

I know this is going to ruffle some feathers and cause some controversy, but I do not believe that there are stages of grief. The stages of grief were originally described in a book called *On Death and Dying* written by Elizabeth Kubler-Ross. The five stages outlined were denial, anger, bargaining, depression, and acceptance. She developed those theories based on a study of terminally ill patients. I am not a psychiatrist or a psychologist, but I could not disagree with the steps more. Saying that everyone *has* steps and that there are five of them is saying that everyone experiences grief the same; in my experience that is just not true. I also think that theory causes grieving people to start to look for what stage they are in, and if the stages are missing, they worry. What if they don't experience all five of the stages? They may think something is wrong or they are not grieving "properly." I do think it was a great book, and it is well worth reading. I will leave it up to you to decide if there are five stages of grief. As for me, I do not believe in them.

Myth number four: Don't make any decisions.

I have heard many people say that when we are in the process of grieving, we shouldn't make any decisions for the first couple of years. I understand the concept, and I do believe that some major decisions should not be made in the first few months. I don't think people should go crazy making massive changes in their life before they're sure that their head is screwed on straight. It would have been bad for me to sell my house and move to Tahiti with a young supermodel. (No really, it would!) However, you will find you will be asked to make a boatload of critically important decisions almost immediately after you've had a loss. You have to decide on funeral arrangements, burials, and many other financial arrangements in fairly quick order.

In the first week after my wife died I had to decide on an autopsy, a viewing (whether to have one or not), the funeral (where, when, and how), and if my wife was going to be buried or cremated. Since then I've had to make a whole host of decisions about everything financially, spiritually, socially, and logistically. The list goes on and on. In a later chapter I will be reviewing with you some of the things that you're going to need to decide on and give you some suggestions on how to make the best possible decisions for you.

Myth number five: Companies that you deal with will have empathy for your situation and will have systems set up to help you as you are grieving.

This could not be further from the truth, and unfortunately, I discovered the opposite. Dealing with my bank to change over my accounts was very painful, laborious, and infuriating. A few days after my wife passed away I went to the bank and had her name removed from both the checking and savings account. I then went home and logged on to my bill pay account for my bank. My wife had been in charge of paying the bills and I wanted to see all of the accounts that were set up so that I could begin taking over that responsibility. Unfortunately, she did not leave me the password for the online checking so I called my bank. I patiently explained to them that my wife had passed away, and I would now be taking care of paying the bills so I needed to get a password reset. After talking to five different people I finally spoke to a supervisor, who told me they could not reset the password, and I would have to set up the bill pay all over again. I was stunned and angry. "I have been banking with you folks forever—I don't understand what the problem is." She explained in a very condescending tone that the bill pay account was not our account, but was Cindy's account and Cindy's alone. They would be happy to reset the account, but when it was reset, the bill pay would be wiped out and I would have to re-set up every account in the system. Resetting up all of the accounts in the system for bill pay took me over five hours. What a headache.

Throughout my experience as a widower I have had many unpleasant dealings with banks, phone companies, credit card companies, clothing companies, retail stores, and catalogs. All of them made it difficult and very laborious to change an account to my name only even though I have great credit. As I said to someone at my giant phone company, they have forgotten about the customer and the customer's experience and are caught up solely in their processes. The only problem is the processes are not set up to handle someone dying. It has been almost two years, and yes, in today's mail I received from my big phone company yet another bill with my late wife's name on it. I have had at least nine discussions with them about the name change on the account, but that just doesn't seem to matter. If I were king of the world, I would make every customer service representative of every company take empathy training, and force companies to develop a process to more empathetically handle the death of someone's loved one.

Myth number six: There is a time frame for grief.

When I worked in corporate America, each company had a bereavement policy. Their bereavement policy often stated that someone would get one week off for the death of a spouse, three days off for the death of a parent, and two days off for the death of some other family member. Where did these numbers come from? How did they arrive at the idea that one week was enough for the death of a spouse, but people only needed three days for the death of a parent? It is a ridiculous concept. Some people grieve quickly and heal quickly; some people grieve slowly and heal slowly. There is no right or wrong answer—everyone has to grieve in their own time. Just don't get caught up in society's view of how long grieving should last.

Let me give you an example from my own life. My wife died in May. In August my best friend Dave was moving from Louisville to Washington, D.C. I flew from my area in Philadelphia to Louisville, Kentucky to help him move. Dave and I have been friends for over 28 years, and he truly is my best friend (as he describes it, "my brother from another mother"). After we had packed the truck and headed on our journey to Washington, D.C., we had many hours to talk in the truck. That was a day that changed my life. Dave wanted to know how I was doing with my grieving and what some of the challenges were that I was facing. I told him that my biggest challenge was dealing with loneliness. He paused and looked at me and said, "So when do you think you'll start dating?"

"Well," I said, "I would but…"

"Would but what?" he said.

"Well, you know, society and all that—what would people, you know—say?"

Dave looked at me and said, "If you are lonely, date. And since when, my buddy, do you let society tell you what you should and should not do? C'mon."

We talked about it for quite a while and he also said that he thought that Cindy would've wanted me to be happy and not lonely. He made some very good points and made me feel as if my instincts about dating was my truth for me. That night we had dinner with his wife, Sara, and Dave asked Sara for her opinion about me dating. She also had a very insightful view (she has always been very smart). She said, "Well, Shawn, in my opinion, people who have been happily married want to be happily married again and in a relationship again and in love again." I really appreciated their friendship, love, and support. They are the best.

On the way back home, I had plenty of time to think about the discussions that we had and decided that I was ready to date. I wanted to give it a try to see how I felt about it, and frankly, how I would feel about being with another woman after 32 years of being with one woman. I mean, how weird would it be? A few weeks later, I went over to have dinner with my daughter and her husband. I told them I was seriously thinking about dating, but the two opinions that mattered the most were theirs. I did not want them to have any ill will or bad feelings about me dating. My daughter, who was 27 at the time, was so supportive and encouraging. She said that she did not want me to be alone, and she wanted me to do what made me happy. I said I did not want to be disrespectful of her mom's memory or for her to think that I was not being loyal. She said very quietly and elegantly, "Dad, when mom was alive you treated her like a queen, that's what everybody says. But the other thing is that you can't be disloyal to someone who has passed away; she is no longer here. Please do what you need to do to be happy, and I will support you."

I know there will be people reading this chapter who will be *outraged* that Shawn Doyle wanted to date after his beloved wife had only been gone for four months. There were people in my family who were not happy and felt it was "too soon." They felt I was trying to replace Cindy. It is *so not* up to them. That's OK with me, if that is how people feel. They have not had to live in my shoes or experienced my life alone. They have not felt the same pain. They don't come home to a heartbreakingly empty house. So I do not judge them for being outraged, but at the same time I hope that they will not stand in judgment of me, because I did what I had to do for me and me alone. I didn't mean to hurt anyone doing it, and I didn't. During the conversation with my daughter, she had also reminded me that I was legally, morally, spiritually, and socially single. That was true, but I had not thought of it that way up to that point. In my book *Jumpstart Your Motivation*, I mentioned the concept of being the architect of your own life. When I decided to start dating, that was a prevailing theme. It was up to me to decide what I wanted my life to be like and not up to anyone else. I did feel truly blessed that I had the support of the most important people in my life, and none of them stood in judgment. In fact it was the opposite; they held me up with love and support and encouraged me. They were my emotional wings and helped me fly.

Myth number seven: You stop grieving.

I am really not sure that anyone ever stops grieving. The way I look at it is the grief will always be with you, it just lessens over time. Grief to me is like a blue balloon. Let me explain what I mean. At first, I was holding the balloon and with string wrapped around my wrist, and it went with me wherever I went. Eventually, with time, the string got longer and longer and longer. One day I went out into the yard of my life and released the balloon into the sky. The balloon, however, did not fly away immediately; it hung around a while, kind of hovering near my head. The balloon gradually started to gain altitude, and each day the balloon was little higher in the sky. Until one day it was just a tiny azure speck in the sky. Some days I see it, and it floats down lower. Some days I don't see it at all. Some days I open a drawer and it is in there. It will never completely disappear, for I carry it with me always. I think grief is like that; it doesn't go away, you just learn to live with it and move on with your life. I promise it is true.

Myth number eight: You should wear your wedding ring for a certain amount of time.

After my wife passed away I often sat in the evenings and wondered how long I should wear my wedding ring. I also knew that one day I would take it off and wondered what I would do with it. Would I put it on a chain around my neck? Store it somewhere in the jewelry box for safekeeping? How long would I wear it? Oh the things we agonize over after a loss.

I stopped wearing my wedding ring about three months after my wife passed away for a very specific reason. I travel a great deal as a professional speaker, and everyone would see my ring and ask me about my wife. They would ask things like, "So how long you been married?" or, "What does your better half do?" It became very awkward and uncomfortable, because I didn't want to explain to a stranger that I was a widower. It just seemed like too much to put on their shoulders after I just met them. So I took my wedding ring off and explained to my family the reasons why. So please don't feel obligated or pressured by friends or family or society to wear your ring for a certain amount of time. It's up to you when you take it off. It's up to you how long you want to wear it. There is no right or wrong answer.

THINGS PEOPLE SAY

In an attempt to comfort me, many people said things which were interesting to say the least. Let me tell you some things I was told and my thoughts about them, in the hope that it may help you.

"His/her spirit is with you."

I had many people in the first few months who told me "I am sure you can feel her spirit is with you." I'm truthful in saying this—I couldn't feel her there—but I did not tell them that. I just gave some polite response. I can't say that some people can't feel the spirit of the dearly departed is with them, it just wasn't true for me. So when people said that, it made me feel a little uncomfortable and awkward because I *didn't* feel her spirit. Was something wrong with me? Was I out of touch? For me it was misinformation that I found confusing and somewhat disturbing. I think it's because the other person is again assuming what I feel or don't feel.

"God needed another angel."

This is not a book about religion or theology, but I do *not* believe that God or Allah or Buddha would snatch someone from their family, causing them a tremendous amount of grief and pain, so that they could be an extra angel in heaven. I don't believe that. That is not the God I believe in. The God I believe in is a kind and loving God.

"I have a message from your wife/husband/loved one."

I had two different occasions when people felt compelled to sit down and talk to me because they felt sincerely that they had received a message from Cindy that she wanted them to deliver to me. I have no doubt these people truly believed they had received a message from my late wife, and I know that they had pure intentions in delivering the message. What I found odd about that situation was that neither one of those people knew my wife or had ever met her. I sat around many evenings scratching my head wondering why my wife would deliver a message to a total stranger and not to someone she had known in life. I decided to reject the idea that my wife was communicating with me from the great beyond. If I'm being honest, I also found it somewhat creepy and disturbing and bothersome. I am still trying to figure why it bothered me. I am not saying what you have to believe. If someone talks to you and says that they have a message from your loved one and you believe it to be true, that is up to you. The other reason that I mention it is that I do not want you to be shocked if it happens to you.

"It was for the best."

There are times when someone is suffered terribly with a terminal disease, such as cancer or leukemia. Because those people at the funeral or memorial service will tell the person who is grieving that the person's death was for the best. I've never known anyone grieving the loss of a loved one who really thought dying was the best outcome. This is another case where people are saying things to try to make you feel better, but often what they say makes you feel a little bit worse. Have mercy on them because they do not know what to say, and they feel very awkward. They are just feeling bad for you.

"You look like you are doing pretty good/you are holding up well."

I am not sure how I was supposed to look—unshaven, pale with red eyes? Disheveled and in my slippers all day? Curled up in a ball? Does the outside of me really say how I am doing? The outside is not in any way an accurate barometer of what is going on inside a person's head. It's kind of an odd comment, and my theory is that they are trying to convince themselves that I am OK because I look normal. I never really knew what to say to that one. If they could have only seen me in bed late at night when I was an emotional wreck—I don't think they would have said it then.

"It was God's will."

I am just a mere mortal, and I have no idea what God's will is. I would not ever question him and his will. But when people said that to me—and it was said a few times—it didn't make me feel better. I thought "Okay, so what if it was God's will She still didn't make it—she died—so do I feel good about that? Nope." What if it wasn't God's will and just an accident? I still felt bad about it. It brought me zero comfort.

MISINFORMATION

Grief only affects you emotionally.

The reality is grief affects you in many ways. The most obvious one is emotionally. I found that grief affected me physically, because in the first week after my wife died, I had absolutely no appetite for food. It affected me spiritually, because it caused me to reconnect with my spirituality. It affected me socially, because the people I socialized with changed after Cindy's death. I went from being married to single. When you're no longer part of a "couple," your social life is affected—not necessarily in a negative way—it just is different. My wife's death also affected me financially and in every other way. Some people make a big mistake of assuming the grief only affects the person grieving in one way. It affects you in many ways.

It's not OK to be happy.

In my mind this is one of the strangest misunderstandings that people have about grieving. Two weeks after my wife passed away, my daughter and her husband invited me to attend an outdoor art show on a beautiful day. I love art, I love being outdoors, and I love being with my daughter and her husband, so I said yes. While attending the art show we saw people we knew, and they obviously knew what had happened to my wife. Some came over quietly and said they were sorry, but at the same time they were looking at me and I could almost see that they were thinking, "Why is he here?" and, "Why does he look so happy?" I don't believe that happiness and grief are mutually exclusive. I can be happy during the day at the art show and sad in the evening being alone at the house. But because I'm grieving doesn't mean that I can't go to the art show and be happy. Life really does move on.

Grieving the death of an infant or a stillborn child is easier.

Some people have the absurd idea that when someone loses a baby or suffers a miscarriage, it is easier to handle than the death of an older child. Ridiculous. I can only say for me it was more tragic, not less. Why more tragic? It was more tragic because there was never a chance for her to live. I had a baby who died as the result of a cord accident before she was born. Lauren Sue Doyle died at eight months, and we never got to know her. She never got the chance. Some people actually assume that you will get over a miscarriage more quickly than you would the death of the two- or three-year-old child. This is a very unfair and cold assumption that people make, and I don't know why they make it. Try not to let these people upset you too much—they just don't know what they're talking about because they have not experienced it.

If I don't grieve long enough or hard enough I didn't love that person as much.

Many times people judge how much you loved the other person by how long you are willing to grieve or how hard you are grieving. Grieving is not a matter of quantity or quality. It is not up to anyone to judge how we grieve. There are some people who decide that they will never marry again after they lose a husband or wife. That is their choice, which I respect. I personally find that to be sad because they will never have a loving relationship again with a husband, wife, or partner. Just because I grieve differently or I fall in love with another person doesn't mean that I loved Cindy any less. I believe that human beings have an unlimited capacity to love, and love doesn't run out. There's no budget for love. So I can love my first wife, and I can get married and love my second wife. The love of the second wife does not cancel out the love of the first. Grief is not something, I feel, that you have to demonstrate to others. It is very personal and private.

Family members will help you.

Some family members were a tremendous help to me during the time that my grieving was the most intense. However, some family members were not helpful, and in fact, they were the opposite. They said and did things that were inappropriate and were not supportive at the time that I needed them the most. I will leave it at that because I don't want to hurt anyone's feelings. Keep in mind that some family members may do things with good intentions, but it will not be helpful for you. It may be hurtful. Some people just lack self-awareness and sensitivity toward others. Just be nice and give them some slack and keep in mind that they are stressed and grieving too.

You should not ever be angry at the one who passed away.

Many people assume that because you're grieving you will never be angry at the one who's passed away. That it would be somehow disrespectful. What's funny about that concept is that if you were frustrated or angry with that person when they were alive, that would be perfectly normal. But because they passed away, now people assume that it would not be appropriate for you to be angry at them. It would be disrespectful. Well guess what? It is OK to be angry at the person who has passed away if you have a reason.

I can tell you there have been times that I have been very angry at my late wife. I have expressed that anger when I have been alone. I told her what I was angry about. You can even be angry at the person because they left you. You can be angry for what they did or didn't do when they were alive. You can be angry at them for the situation they may have put you in by passing away. I think being angry is actually a healthy approach because it helps you burn off any frustration or anger that you may have. So if you are feeling guilty about being angry at a loved one—don't be. It is a normal human emotion, and I am sure if they were alive they would understand. Cut yourself some slack—this isn't an easy journey, and don't add to it by being hard on yourself.

You have all the answers.

You don't, you won't, and you probably never will. There have been so many questions people have asked me over the last 22 months. Am I going to keep the house? Move? Get married? Stay single? Change occupations? The answer to all those questions at various times has been, "I don't know." There were times I didn't even know what I was going to do the next day, the next week, or the next month. I think it is OK to say you don't have the answers and just be OK with it. Just let it be for a while.

A death after a prolonged illness is the same as a sudden death.

I don't think they are the same. My wife did not know she was going to die when she did, so we didn't get to say anything to one another. There were no goodbyes. People with terminal illnesses do get a chance to have those kinds of discussions. I think in case of a terminal illness the grieving process starts when the person is still alive. I am not saying it makes it easier—I am just saying it is very different.

The person doesn't want to talk about the loved one they lost.

Many people visited me at my house and didn't know what to say. They didn't know if I wanted to talk about Cindy and what happened. Some people want to talk about it and some don't. If you are grieving, you make the rules. If you don't want to talk about it—don't. If you want to talk about it—feel free.

So those are some myths and misunderstandings you will face when grieving. Just know that most people will have your best interest in mind, and they just feel really bad for you. They want to take away your pain and they can't. Keep that at the front of your mind and maintain a sense of humor if you can—it helps.

> "Isn't it weird," I said, "the way you remember things, when someone's gone?"
>
> "What do you mean?"
>
> I ate another piece of waffle. "When my dad first died, all I could think about was that day. It's taken

me so long to be able to think back to before that, to everything else."

Wes was nodding before I even finished. "It's even worse when someone's sick for a long time," he said. "You forget they were ever healthy, ever OK. It's like there was never a time when you weren't waiting for something awful to happen."

"But there was," I said. "I mean, it's only been in the last few months that I've started remembering all this good stuff, funny stuff about my dad. I can't believe I ever forgot it in the first place."

"You didn't forget," Wes said, taking a sip of his water. "You just couldn't remember right then. But now you're ready to, so you can."

I thought about this as I finished off my waffle.

—Sarah Dessen, *The Truth about Forever*

CHAPTER 3

HOPE AND ASSURANCE

*"There is neither happiness nor misery in the world;
there is only the comparison of one state with
another, nothing more. He who has felt the deepest
grief is best able to experience supreme happiness.
We must have felt what it is to die, Morrel, that
we may appreciate the enjoyments of living. Live,
then, and be happy, beloved children of my heart,
and never forget, that until the day God shall deign
to reveal the future to man, all human wisdom is
summed up in these two words—'Wait and Hope.'"*
—ALEXANDRE DUMAS, *The Count of Monte Cristo*

I AM SURE RIGHT NOW YOU ARE GRIEVING AND DEVASTATED. I am sure right now you don't even think there is a light at the end of the tunnel or there is even a tunnel at all. I come bearing good news. I hold the lantern of hope and I am shining it on you. Do you feel the warmth? There is hope. I can tell you that there is hope because I have lived through losing a child and a wife. You can have hope for happiness in the future. I promise.

I have a very clear recollection of sitting many nights in my living room alone in an empty house reading a book or watching TV. I felt very lonely and sad, and I remember thinking, "OK, it has been two months since my wife passed away. How will I be in a year from now? How will I feel 18 months from now? What will my life be like?" It was almost as if I was having an out-of-body experience, but I was thinking about how I was thinking. I hoped for a bright future, but I wasn't sure how I was going to get through grief to get to the other side of my life. But I always had the sliver of hope and optimism. So the purpose of this particular chapter is to let you know that there is a future ahead of you, and I think you can have a bright and hopeful future where you can eventually be happy again. I am living proof of this concept.

So let me give you some general concepts to think about as you are grieving, and ones that I hope will give you optimism as you look toward the future.

You are going to be OK.

I just wanted to let you know that despite your tragedy and your loss you will eventually be OK. I can't tell you how long that will be or how it will happen. I can only give you tools, tips, and techniques in order to help you on your journey. I hope you will find these valuable for you. When I talked to my uncle Scott in California about two weeks after my wife passed away, the first thing he said to me on the phone call was, "You're going to be OK." I thought to myself as he said this, "How could he possibly know that I was going to be OK? Maybe after all, I was going to fall apart or be severely depressed or not be able to pull my life back together." After speaking with him for a while, I realized as a pastor he not only had a massive amount of experience delivering sermons, performing weddings, and ministering to his church members, but he also had a tremendous amount of experience counseling people who were going through the grief process and conducting funerals. So I believed him. Now as you read this, I want you to believe me—you are going to be OK. Yes, you will face trials and tribulations. You have several obstacles to face as you go through the grief process, but I believe that believing you're going to be OK is the first step. Believe it—you will be.

One of the things that comforted me during my early days of grieving was reading books about grief. Although that sounds morbid, it was a tremendous help because I discovered that I was not alone. I became an avid student of grief literature, carefully reading each book. There were, after all, many other people on the planet who experienced the tragedy and loss that I had experienced as well, and they shared how they handled it. So it was a tremendous comfort to me just to know that I was not alone in what I was experiencing. I don't know if you know this or not, but according to statistics about 2.5 million people die in the United States every year. So you aren't alone—many are experiencing what you're experiencing. I want you to try to adjust your thought process and say to yourself, either out loud or just thinking it, that *you are going to be OK*. Make it an affirmation. Say it to yourself several times a day and you will believe it.

You can survive and thrive.

I know that sounds like somewhat of an arrogant comment. Let me explain what I mean. I survived the death of my wife, and I believe it has made me a better person and a stronger person, which has allowed me to not only survive but *thrive.* For example, maybe in the past I would get ready to do something and I would delay or put it off. I now have learned that life is short, so I'm going to live life to the fullest. If there's something I want to do, I don't delay or put it off. I am all about seizing the day!

If I love someone, like my mom or my dad, when I'm talking on the phone the last thing I say to them is "I love you." I tell them that because I realize that there will be a time when I may not be able to tell them. Life is so short. So having survived the grieving and tragedy has allowed me to see the world through different-colored glasses, and they are the glasses of appreciation for life. I see the good not the bad. I no longer worry about the small things because I realize the small things don't matter, and only certain things truly matter. The rest are just minor irritations. My uncle also gave me another concept which really struck me. When you experience loss, it certainly is a tragedy. There are many negatives about the loss, no question about that. But as terrible as it sounds, the loss can also offer certain freedoms or opportunities that you would not have had otherwise.

Please don't misinterpret this—I'm not suggesting for a second that I wished for my wife to pass away. Her dying created a lot of loss in my life in so many ways, which I had no control over whatsoever. The flip side of the equation is there were also certain opportunities that were created. Before getting offended by this comment, please think about it. For example, if I decided six months after my wife passed away that I wanted to go to Paris, I could. If I wanted to do A or B or C or D, I had complete autonomy and independence to do so. I was no longer part of a marriage where we discussed and decided things together. All decisions were now just my own. Please don't miss this point—it's so very important. Please, whatever you do, don't feel guilty for having the freedom or enjoying parts of it. You didn't choose it, you didn't ask for it, but it is a reality. So it certainly is something to think about.

You can reinvent your life.

I realized after my wife passed away that my life had changed forever and she was never coming back. That very sad permanence is probably the most disturbing aspect of someone dying. A couple of weeks after my wife passed away, I started to think about what I wanted my life to be now that I was living a life without Cindy. I had the opportunity to redraw the entire blueprint of my life. I could reinvent the work that I did, where I lived, who I socialized with, and any other aspect of my life socially, mentally, spiritually, financially, and logistically.

The first thing I did was decide that I needed to lose weight. I thought that the intense focus and concentration of dieting and working out would help me lose weight, have more energy, and feel better about myself. So I literally reinvented myself physically. I signed up for Weight Watchers, followed the nutrition plan very carefully, and worked out on a regular and consistent basis. The good news is I lost a total of 54 pounds and 9 inches in my waist. The act of reinventing myself physically was a tremendous boost to my energy level, and I felt much better about my image as a person. So when you feel ready, I want you to take the time to look at all of the areas of your life and which of those areas you would like to change or reinvent. Redraw your life blueprint from this point forward. I also believe that the act of reinvention is an act of hope and optimism because it makes everything in life brand-new. After all, you can't have the old, so here comes the new.

I also have to give credit to Jai Pausch who wrote the book *Dream New Dreams: Reimagining My Life After Loss*. You may recognize her last name; she is the widow of the world-famous, late Professor Randy Pausch who wrote the book *The Last Lecture*. You may have seen his "last lecture" on the Internet. He was an insightful man. To me one of the key concepts in her book was the idea of reimagining your life or as I refer to it *reinventing* your life. Think of it as taking your life and pushing the reset button. You had a life with the person you lost (we can call that "life one") and now you have a new life without that person (we call that "life two") and can decide what you want that life to be.

Looking at it in this way can actually be an exciting concept. I also think that it is extremely healthy to realize that I will never have "life one" again. "Life one," sadly, is over. You can acknowledge it, love it, remember it, cherish it, but it's gone. So now you can march boldly forward and embrace "life two." If you take the right approach and attitude, it can be very exciting. Also, please don't feel guilty about "life two." This is not a path that you chose. You were put into a circumstance that you have no control over at all. But the one thing you do have control over is how you respond to it and what your life is going to look like in the next phase. Yes, you could be miserable for years and years, and if you make that choice, that's OK. However, I think you can again live a rich, rewarding, and happy life by deciding to embrace your new life and reinvent yourself. We are the only species in the world, as far as I know, that has the ability to think about our life and to reinvent it. I have never seen a deer decide to be a buffalo or a turtle decide to be a fish. I have, however, seen many people in this lifetime who completely and utterly reinvented themselves in a positive way after massive tragedy and loss. You can too!

This is trial and error.

I lost my wife on May 4. Saturday, May 5 when I woke up in the morning, I was suddenly single and a widower. I found this to be a very odd, uncomfortable label after being married for 32 years. I didn't know what it meant to be single. I didn't know what it meant to be a widower. I didn't even know what I didn't know. So I decided that it would be OK not to know anything and that my life for the next year would be a series of trial and error, where some things would work and some things wouldn't. I was prepared for awkwardness. A couple of months after my wife passed away, a female friend of mine called and asked if I wanted to have dinner with her. She was single and I was single, and she was a very nice person. I talked to her several times on the phone and we agreed to meet and have dinner. For some strange reason, though, I told her that I would have dinner with her, "but it wasn't like it was a date or anything." She said, "of course it wasn't." I don't know why, but I felt very awkward about the entire thing.

What did single people do when they were having dinner? What if she asked me to have drinks afterward? What if she invited me to come over to her house to talk? I even called my daughter and explained to her that I was having dinner with a woman and did not want her to get the wrong idea, in case she saw me at the restaurant (as if I was cheating or something). My daughter said she appreciated me telling her, but it really was OK for me to have dinner with anyone I wanted to have dinner with. My friend agreed to have dinner with me on our "non-date." I was a nervous wreck driving there on the way to having dinner.

When we finally had dinner, she was poking fun at me for labeling it as a non-date. She then told me that any time two single people get together for dinner and one is male and one is a female that it is technically "a date." That also threw me for a loop. As it turns out we had a very nice dinner and good, fun conversation. I did feel awkward and out of place because it was such a foreign experience after having been married for so long. I was a fish way out of water.

So why do I bring this up? Because as you go through life grieving, there will be times you'll feel clumsy, awkward, and out of place. The key is to get through it and move on, and eventually you won't feel awkward and out of place. You will adjust quite nicely. When I think back on those times now, I kind of chuckle at how silly I was to label it as a "non-date." What a clumsy new single man I was. I had been married for 32 years and didn't know how dating even worked any more. What was dating anyway?

There will sometimes not be an answer.

In the famous Beatles song *Let It Be,* there is a line that says, "There will be an answer, let it be." I am here to tell you there will be many times you will not have an answer. I have learned to be OK with that, because there aren't any. My wife died of a brain aneurism at the young age of 50. Why? I don't know. The coroner said it could have been a congenital defect, but the kind of aneurism she had destroys itself when it bursts. So he said he could say without a doubt that was the cause of death, but couldn't say why she died at 50 years old and not, say, 70 years old or 30 years old.

Why do some people die young and others of old age? Why do good people die and bad people live? I don't know. Why are people married 60 years and I only had 32? Why did I lose a wife and so many people still have them? I don't know. I don't know. I don't know. The *why* will never be answered, ever. So I just want you to know there will be many unanswered questions and you just have to at some point be OK with thinking, "Well…there is no answer." It's part of the great mystery of life.

The pain will get better with time.

You are in pain and will be in pain. That is the bad news. The good news is the pain will get better with time, and one day it will actually go away. How can I say that? I can say that because I lived through the pain, every minute of it. In the beginning I was in a tremendous amount of pain while grieving the loss of my wife. Each day when I got up I realized yet again that she was not here, and that was incredibly painful. I will tell you though, that each day the pain got to be a little less, then a little less, then a little less, until one day I had an entire day when I did not think about the grief, and I was not in pain. Now don't get me wrong—at the writing of this book it has been 22 months and there still are times that I am in pain or grieving. However, the space between the times that I am in pain or not in pain continues to grow in distance. I can't say for you what the time frame will be for your pain. I can only share with you how I have healed, and the majority of days I feel no pain of grieving at all. I still carry the experience of the loss with me, but the pain has faded.

You are stronger than you realize.

I always thought of myself as a reasonably strong person and someone who was optimistic. I realize having gone through the trials and tribulations of grief has made me a much stronger person, but also led me to a realization that I already was a strong person. I just didn't know it. Many people have said they have been inspired by my strength and the way that I have handled my grief. I can only say that I have tried the best I can each day, and that's all that I can do. You may seriously think to yourself, "I just can't take this," or, "This is the worst thing that has ever happened in my life." My response is that I agree with you—it is the worst thing that has ever happened in your life, but you can take it. You are much stronger than you know. You really don't know how much steel you have in your spine until it is tested. Then you realize you really are very strong. As Eleanor Roosevelt once said:

You gain strength, courage, and confidence by every experience in which you really stop to look fear in the face. You are able to say to yourself, "I have lived through this horror. I can take the next thing that comes along." You must do the thing you think you cannot do.

I have learned for myself that because I went through this time of tragedy and grief, it made me stronger for handling other problems or challenges that I have faced since then. It is almost as if you build up some emotional muscle to use when you need it.

You have resources.

I was very fortunate to have the loving support of many friends and family members during the early days of my grief. I remember calling my best friend Dave one night around nine o'clock in the evening and telling him that I was really struggling with loneliness. Talking to him made me feel better. He understood and gave me lots of great suggestions and ideas. Mary Kelly, a fellow professional speaker, heard through one of our mutual friends that I had lost my wife. She was a widow who lost her husband about seven years before. She was kind enough to write me an e-mail saying that she was sorry for my loss and if I needed any advice to feel free to contact her. One night did call her. We exchanged stories and she gave me some great advice. Throughout the last 22 months I have been absolutely astounded at the people who have called, e-mailed, visited, sent me a message on Facebook, or sent a text message to my phone, just to let me know that they were thinking of me and supporting me. So you do have resources in friends and family who can certainly help comfort you and advise you during your time of grief. Lean on them for a while, embrace them, and ask them for help. There is nothing wrong with that.

I would like to give you a quick heads-up for something to watch out for. Make sure that you pick the right advisors who will help you and not hurt you; who will be optimistic, not pessimistic; and who will raise you up, not bring you down. I'm not saying that any of these people will do that on purpose, but you have to be extremely careful to protect yourself. You are vulnerable during the time that you're grieving. Be careful not to expose yourself to toxic, negative people. There are also many books, support groups, websites, and other great resources that can help you during a most difficult time. They can bring you comfort, advice, and ideas. I have listed as many of these resources as possible in the back of the book for you to use as tools to help you heal. Try them out.

You can choose your attitude.

OK, I know you're probably irritated reading this. How do you choose to have a positive attitude when you've lost a wife, husband, child, or some other relative or friend? "What's there to be happy about?" the cynic may ask. I have a confession: two weeks after my wife passed away I conducted my first live training program. Why would I choose to run a full-day training program when my wife had only passed away two weeks before? Well, it's simple. I decided I was not going to sit around the house and be miserable all day long. So I got up in the morning feeling very miserable, led the training during the day and felt great (I love and have a passion for what I do), and then in the evening felt sad again. Here is the key point: for eight hours that day I was able to be in a happy state of connecting with other human beings in a training program. I say there's nothing wrong with that. The late Zig Ziglar once said, "If your thinking is stinking—then you need to get a checkup from the neck up." Yes, this is quite a humorous quote, but I like the idea of it. I choose how I think and I choose my attitude. Six weeks after my wife passed away, I went to Hersheypark by myself for the day. Many people thought I had lost my mind. "Why are you going to Hersheypark?" they asked. My answer was simple: "Amusement parks make me happy." Enough said.

Why would I have a positive attitude even though I'm a widower who suffered a tragic loss? I think that is an interesting question and a lot depends on your perspective. I could sit around and say, "I can't believe that my wife died; it is so unfair." Or I could just say that I'm grateful that I was married to her for 32 years. I could say that I'm grateful for my health, I'm grateful that my wife did not suffer, I'm grateful for the fact that I was home with her when she died so she did not die alone. I think my daughter Alexis said it best; she said she was just glad she had a mom who saw her through school, got to see her graduate from high school and college, and got to attend her wedding. She said if her mom had died sooner, then at all those events she would've been thinking about her mom. So she said she was grateful to have had her mom as long as she did, even though she wished she would've been around longer. So there are many things to be grateful for, but we don't take the time to sit down and think through them.

I would advise writing out a list—not of all the things you're mourning or grieving—but for all the things you're grateful for. Let's say you actually suffered the tragedy of losing a very young child who was only a few years old. What possibly would there be to be grateful for? There are many things, I imagine. We could say we are grateful we have the rest of our family. We could say we were grateful to have had them as long as we did. We could say we were lucky that they did not suffer. So in almost any tragic situation there are still things that we can say we are grateful for.

Beyond being grateful, I'm just going to decide to have a happy attitude about life. To me, life is so short and precious that I'm not going to waste my life sitting around being miserable, mean, and sad. So I will choose for me to have a positive, upbeat attitude. About three weeks after my wife passed away, I was visiting an art gallery in my area. The manager of the gallery greeted me, welcomed me to the gallery, and showed me some work that they were displaying. We got into an in-depth conversation and I told him that I was thinking about getting into collecting art. I was still wearing my wedding ring at the time and he asked me how my wife felt about the idea of collecting art. I told him that I was a widower and my wife had passed away three weeks ago. I didn't mean to, but my comment almost knocked the poor man off of his feet. At first, he was speechless. Then he said, "I just can't believe that you're a widower and you're only a widower now for three weeks. You seem to have such a great, upbeat attitude." I told him that it was not easy, but I decided to maintain a positive attitude as much as I could most of the time.

Don't get me wrong; I have had days where I honestly felt sorry for myself. I have felt sorry for my daughter and her husband and my sister-in-law and all the other family members and friends who experienced the loss of my wife. But those days are few and far between, and I don't believe that I should waste my time on earth feeling miserable and sorry for myself. I choose to move forward. I choose to be optimistic. I choose to heal, honor the past, but embrace the present. I look forward to the future. This is what I choose. It's funny; I've written several books about motivation in my career as a professional speaker. The biggest question that anyone might legitimately ask me is, "Well, I wonder what his attitude will be like when he faces adversity." I wondered about that myself in the early days, and I made a decision—I was not going to live my life being miserable, and that is, I firmly believe, a choice. I can decide to be happy or I can decide to be miserable.

To close this chapter I think this quote is profound:

> There is so much about my fate that I cannot control, but other things do fall under the jurisdiction. I can decide how I spend my time, whom I interact with, whom I share my body and life and money and energy with. I can select what I can read and eat and study. I can choose how I'm going to regard unfortunate circumstances in my life—whether

I will see them as curses or opportunities. I can choose my words and the tone of voice in which I speak to others. And most of all, I can choose my thoughts.

—ELIZABETH GILBERT, *Eat, Pray, Love*

CHAPTER 4

COPING, GRIEVING, AND HEALING

"I am determined to be cheerful and happy in whatever situation I may find myself. For I have learned that the greater part of our misery or unhappiness is determined not by our circumstance but by our disposition." —MARTHA WASHINGTON

ONCE THE FUNERAL WAS OVER, RESPECTS HAD BEEN PAID, the noise had died down, and family members all went back home, I was now trying to figure out how to cope. How do you cope with such a major catastrophic life change? The problem is that everyone else goes back to their life, to work, to their families, and to their homes. Meanwhile, I had a life, but what was it? It was inalterably changed. I still had my work, but I no longer had my family as I defined it, and my home had become very empty and lonely. It's not as if the people who went home had forgotten about you, but I do think they forget how your life is as a person who is living loss on a daily basis. Everything changed. You know how you lived in the "before"—but how do you live in the "after"?

So I will share with you in this chapter the tools and techniques that I used in order to cope and grieve and heal.

A GRIEF EDUCATION

May of that year was extremely difficult and I was grieving, but I knew that I needed to start working toward coping and healing. I've always believed in education and information. So my first step was to get an education in grief. My education in grief consisted of two main approaches:

1. Talking to people who have had significant loss themselves; particularly someone who lost a spouse.

2. Reading books about grief and grieving.

It would give me ideas and allow me to think through what I was experiencing. One of the reasons I decided to read books about grief is that I thought that maybe several other people had experienced what I had experienced, so they had ideas and ways to deal with intense grief.

My very dear friend Joe Townsend was a pilot who lost his wife and children in a plane crash many years ago. I ended up writing a book about Joe and his tragedy called *The Soul Survivor*. So I authored a book about Joe's experience of losing his wife and then leaned on Joe, as my coach when I was grieving after losing my wife, to run ideas and thoughts by him. He was very generous in spending time with me on the phone, giving me ideas, and letting me vent. He also was able to confirm that what I was thinking was "normal" and, on occasion, that I was not losing my mind. He was a great friend and his calm and cheerful demeanor was very helpful to me during that time.

So my advice is to seek out people in your social circles who may have experienced your kind of loss, because they immediately understand where you're coming from and what you are thinking. It's really nice to talk to someone who "gets it" and understands, but more importantly you feel that they understand. Seek these people out, and don't be shy to ask them for help. I found the majority of people I asked for help during my most difficult time were more than willing to help and were so very kind.

I had help from many other people, although those people don't know that they helped me, because they came to me in the form of a book. I decided to find many titles on grief and grieving and read them, digest them, and study them. Overall, I think I read over a dozen, and although sometimes the books about tragedy were sad, they were useful because of the suggestions for healing they contained. I have to say that I found these books extremely helpful because they were real and relevant. So think of yourself as getting a BA in grief and grief-coping skills. There is a famous axiom out there that says *knowledge is power*, but I don't agree with that statement. What I do agree with is *the application of knowledge is power*. So I recommend not only reading books on grief, (please see an additional resource list in the back of this book) but also, after reading through a book once, to go back and take notes and then ask yourself how you can apply this to your life. Then create an action plan for applying them as soon as possible.

THE JOY LIST

The next thing I did probably sounds insane to most people, but I really never cared too much about what other people think because sometimes people just lack creativity. What is the joy list? My thought was that I was obviously in a tremendous amount of pain and I was grieving and dealing with the loss of a loved one. So I would say that could be known as the "sad list." The "sad list" was filled with all of the activities that I had to do which were sad. For example, several weeks after my wife's funeral, the funeral director called me and said that the urn of my wife's cremated remains was ready to be picked up. It was a short drive to the funeral home to pick up the urn but a very sad one. Contacting friends we could not locate to let them know about Cindy's death was sad. Closing credit card accounts and changing bank accounts was sad. Sad activities were central in my life for several months which, let's face it, can be depressing. So I decided to overcome all of the sadness to create a joy list.

The joy list is very simple. It is just a list of all the things that make me happy, bring me up, put me in a good frame of mind, or things that just bring me joy. My thought was if I could plan each week to do some of the things that brought me joy, it would help balance out some of the sad things I had to do that were on the sad list. My joy list included some of the following items:

- Travel

- Art and art museums
- Water parks
- Being with friends
- Hiking
- Drawing and painting
- Working out
- Playing the drums
- Movies
- Shopping
- Amusement parks

So I noticed once I started to work items from my joy list into my weekly schedule—I'm sure this is no surprise—they brought me joy. It felt good to have some joy. More importantly, while I was doing them they brought me joy and I was not thinking about the grief. It was a tremendous boost to my morale. So I would feel sad, I would go do something joyful, and then later that day I might have felt sad again. My point is I didn't feel sad when I was in joy. Now the cynics of the world will say to me, "Well sir, how can you have joy when your wife just died? How can you go anywhere and have fun when you should be grieving?" Well, I say that is nonsense! Just because I worked some moments of joy into my life did not mean that I was not grieving, and it did not mean that I was not missing my wife. I was miserable enough grieving—why would I want to sit around and continue to be miserable? I never understood that mindset. So as for me, I choose joy, I choose happiness, I choose to celebrate life because life is short. I am sure there are some folks reading this book who will say, "Well, that is a great idea to do the joy list—but to be brutally honest, I don't feel like having joy." I understand, I really do. The timing of incorporating the joy list is entirely up to you, or you can never try it at all. I'm going to strongly recommend that you do it anyway.

As I mentioned in a previous chapter, six weeks after my wife died I went to an amusement park. I found that it did help me tremendously to get out and do things that brought me joy. I'm not saying it is a right approach for you. I'm only saying that worked for me. I also believe that when you are grieving sometimes you have to "fake it until you make it." It's almost as if you have to battle your mind—your mind wants to grieve, but your body and your spirit want to go out and play. What I noticed is when I put my body into action (like standing in a wave pool), my body convinced my mind to relax and have fun. So sometimes the mind follows the body and other times the body follows the mind. Just give it a try. Here is a bigger question I would ask anyone—what is so wrong with being happy?

Another advantage of making a joy list is it forces you in some ways to schedule activities instead of just sitting around the house being stagnant and sad. You don't have to do the items on the joy list by yourself—you can invite friends and family to join you if you like. For example, my daughter and her husband went with me to a wonderful art museum, and we not only had the joy of art but the joy of being together.

THE BEACH RETREAT

For a couple months after my wife passed away, I had been thinking about going to some sort of retreat. In August (four months after my wife passed away) I booked four days in Rehoboth Beach, Delaware. It was not a vacation, it was not an escape, it was what I referred to as a retreat. Now what do I mean by retreat? I felt I had gotten to a certain point where I needed to just sit back and process everything that I had gone through and experienced over the last four months. Clear my head and kind of reevaluate where I was and what I was doing. When I told friends and family that I was going away to the beach for four days, their first question was, "By yourself?" Of course the answer was yes. They asked me the purpose of my beach visit and I told them I was going to a retreat. I think there were a few people who thought I'd gone a little bit off the deep end (but that's OK). I decided before I went to the beach that I was not going to socialize, I was not going to talk to anyone except to check into my hotel and order meals. Each day I went for a long walk on the beach in the morning and in the late afternoon, and I sat on the beach each day in a beach chair with an umbrella and just thought for hours and hours. Even though I was surrounded by people, it seemed as if I was in my own little space surrounded by my favorite sights and sounds of the ocean. It was almost as if I went away to a mountaintop monastery or a log cabin in the woods. During that time I also wrote a journal of everything that I had experienced over the last three months. I wrote to my wife and poured out my heart. I wrote everything that I wanted to say to her that I did not get to say. I told her what I was sorry for; I told her what I wish we had done. I told her that I was sorry she had experienced such a bad childhood and was in pain. I told her what I was sad about. I told her what I was angry about and what I didn't understand. This was all in writing. I sat in my chair wearing a baseball hat and dark glasses, crying much of the time. Because it was hot and I was sweating and had on the sunglasses, no one knew I was crying. I cried buckets of tears that week.

I was so glad that I decided to take the retreat to the beach. I felt like I got a lot of issues resolved and settled in my head, and was able to properly frame everything that had happened. The retreat was truly for me a transformational experience. I came back from my trip with a lighter load, clear thinking, and I just felt so much better. I called my daughter on the way home to tell her that I was on my way back. When she asked how my trip went, I told her, "I don't know how to explain this, but I feel a thousand percent better." So the retreat was very cathartic for me. One of the things you might want to strongly think about if you have suffered a loss is to schedule a retreat for you. Pick a favorite place and geography that you find beautiful and peaceful, and go there with the express purpose of just thinking, meditating, praying, reflecting on your loss.

I also strongly recommend that you do journaling during that time to process your thoughts. Take a notebook and a couple of pens and pour out your thoughts and emotions and heart on the paper. Just dump out everything you're thinking, feeling, and processing since your loss. It made a big positive difference for me. If for some reason you're not in the position to be able to go away for a retreat, you can certainly do the same thing locally. You can go for a hike into the woods, stay out all day, sit by a lake in an isolated area, or go up in the mountains. The idea is just to be surrounded by beauty and nature and not distracted by people, phones, computers, and e-mails.

DIET AND EXERCISE

I did decide to go on a diet and work out on a regular, consistent basis not long after my wife passed away. This is something else I would also highly recommend. When you are eating properly, you feel healthier and you feel better about yourself physically. When you are working out and getting in shape, you feel better about yourself mentally and physically. I personally find that when I work out it also gives me a tremendous amount of energy, because I found grieving to be a physically draining activity and it made me very tired. But the working out helps me maintain my level of energy. An additional benefit of working out, as you know, is when you work out your body releases several chemicals which are actually natural mood lifters and help you be more positive. Make a list of all of the kinds of exercises you enjoy doing or maybe consider buying fitness equipment or joining a local gym. Exercise may give you just the boost that you need during a trying and difficult time.

SUPPORT SYSTEM

It is very important to identify who your support system will be. They may friends, family, or even acquaintances. Your support system could also include psychiatrists, psychologists, other doctors as well as ministers, priests, and rabbis. Keep in mind, when it comes to who you need for support, there are no right or wrong answers. Some people may seek out religious or spiritual support or may choose to spend time with a grief counselor or a psychiatrist or psychologist. All that counts is what works for you at that time. I never felt the need to go to a mental health professional because I felt like I was handling it well, but that does not mean that I do not endorse the idea of a counselor if you need one. I had several great support people who helped me through a most difficult time. They were available to talk to me when I called on the phone, or they contacted me to invite me to dinner, or posted messages to me on Facebook or e-mail, or sent me a card in the mail. This small team of people was a huge help to me in supporting me when I needed it most. My suggestion is to make a list of who your support system should be so that when you are feeling down and out, you know who to call or contact without having to think about it. Write the prescription before you need it.

LIVE SOCIAL GROUPS

A friend of mine suggested that I join a social group in my area. The group I joined was a group made up of Chester County (the county that I live in Pennsylvania) widows and widowers. To be clear, it was set up not as a dating group but just as a group to help widows and widowers get together and socialize. They would plan visits to the movies, museums, or lunches and dinners where people could go solo yet feel comfortable being with a group. This group was very helpful because I got to socialize with other widows and widowers without feeling like it was a dating group. I once went on a hike with six other people on a Saturday afternoon and we had a lot of fun. It was also a nice feeling to talk to other widows and widowers on the hike. We had so much fun that one woman in our group invited us all back to her condominium for dinner and to watch a movie. So it is a great way to socialize without any pressure, and to meet nice people. I found my group on meetup.com. Just so you know, Meet Up is a website listing groups organized by different types of people. The groups meet frequently, often with several events each week. The groups can be organized by lifestyle, hobby, gender, or even a particular interest. I found belonging to a group to be helpful in the early days of my grief. So you might want to find groups like that to belong to where you're able to socialize with people without any of the dating pressure.

ONLINE SOCIAL GROUPS

You may already know this but there are over 2 million widow support groups listed online, and the same number of groups for widowers. Some groups gather live, like the Meet Up groups that I mentioned in the last section. There are groups, however, that only meet online and provide forums and chats for people to discuss their loss with other people who have had loss as well. I did not personally get involved with online grief groups myself, but I highly recommend getting involved to see if you like them or if they are helpful to you. This again is just another way to have dialogue with somebody else who understands what you're going through or has been through what you are going through now.

GET BETTER BY GIVING BACK

One of the ways of feeling better about yourself is to serve others who may be less fortunate. I felt the strong need to give back in the midst of my grief. My publisher, Sound Wisdom, was very involved in a charity that ran a bereavement camp for children, called Camp Koala. It is a camp for kids who have lost a parent or a sibling. As soon as they mentioned children and grief, I was hooked because it was so close to my heart. So I asked them how I could help and I became a "big buddy" during camp to a grieving young man. So for three days, my buddy and I did everything together. I participated in healing circles where kids told stories about how they lost their loved one, as did I. Many of the stories involved deaths that were a result of violence and/or drugs, and hearing it from the mouths of children was incredibly tragic to hear. It was painful, poignant, and beautiful. We participated in many fun activities and many healing activities over the weekend, and it did seem to be transformational for the kids. I saw kids come to camp on Friday and leave camp on Sunday feeling much lighter. They seemed like they were kids again. My kid (I won't mention his name) was also able to relate to me because I had lost my wife and he had lost his father. So I guess I had credibility with him. The camp exhausted me both physically and emotionally, and it was hard to experience; however, it made me feel great to make a difference in so many kids' lives in one short weekend. I am now committed and will volunteer to work at the camp every year. So giving back was a healing experience for me and a healing experience for those I was able to work with.

The "giving back" for you does not have to be working in a grief environment, such as a children's bereavement camp or hospice. It could be working at an old folk's home, teaching someone to read, working in a food kitchen, or volunteering with any charity or organization. But I honestly believe that giving back heals you while it heals others. I assure you that I learned just as much from the kids as they did from me.

THE PHYSICAL SPACE

A very good friend of mine, Nathan, sent me a book called *Changing Rooms* which was about a different way of handling grief. The book outlines the importance of signaling that you are making changes in your life by changing your space to help in the healing from your loss. After carefully reading the book, I found this to be a very fascinating concept and made some changes.

I love all things nautical, so I decided to go with a nautical theme. I didn't change any of the furniture, but I did take everything off of the walls in the living room, dining room, and bedroom. I hung new pictures in the living room and the bedroom with the nautical theme and replaced the bedroom linens on the bed. I bought new items to put on the coffee table in the living room. I also repainted my front door a completely different color. Let me tell you, just by making the smallest cosmetic changes, the house seemed like it came back alive again.

Friends came over and thought that I changed all of my furniture in the living room. When I came home from a trip it just seemed like the house was fresh and new. It physically symbolized that I was on to a new life and things were not the same. I found that to be a huge psychological benefit. It's like the house was all "ours" in the way it was decorated. After I re-decorated the house, it was more just "mine." Somehow that also seemed OK too. It was like the house was now in "life two" as well.

So I want you to think about possibly making some changes in some of the spaces in your house. The timing is up to you. I made those changes about three months after my wife passed away. You may want to take longer. There is nothing wrong with that either.

So what will you change? Maybe it's the living room and dining room or your bedroom, but you would be amazed how simple changes in a room's decor can brighten your mood.

Do What You Want to Do

I know that all of our life we have been raised not to be selfish. We should care for others and consider other people's feelings. I think that is absolutely the right idea and way to live. I try to live my life in that way. However, I do believe that when you are in a grieving phase, you should be selfish. You should think very carefully about what you want to do and what you don't want to do. If you don't feel like doing something, don't do it. If you feel like doing something, then do it.

This is the one time in your life that you need to be selfish in order to take care of you. Because I have a fairly good level of self-confidence, I trusted all my instincts during my most difficult grieving period. It was as if sonar was beeping in a direction, and rather than ignoring it, I listened to it. It always served me well. So take time to listen to that inner voice which tells you what you want to do and what you don't want to do. During your most difficult time don't allow people to force you to do anything. Trust your gut.

DON'T APOLOGIZE

I see people all the time who are in grief and are always apologizing to other people who are not in grief. For example, if a person who has suffered a loss starts crying because something reminded them of their loved one, they apologize and say, "Gee, I'm sorry I am crying." Please don't apologize for grieving—it is a natural human emotion and there's no reason to apologize. Most of the time, we are able to control our emotions. Grief is a funny emotion because it will often sneak up on you when you least expect it. You may hear a song on the radio or smell the smell of a certain flower or taste a taste that immediately reminds you strongly of your loved one. This may cause you to choke up or cry or just be sad. If people around you are bothered by the fact that you are crying or choked up—that's their problem not yours—don't apologize.

AVOID NEGATIVE CONTENT

Unfortunately, as you know we live in a very negative world. Negative gets ratings and generates an audience. The world is chock-full of negative news stories, negative people, negative movies, negative TV, negative radio, and lots of sad stuff and it is all around us. One of the rules that I set for myself for about the first six months was that I was not going to expose myself to any negativity. Man, my wife had died—that was negative enough. My daughter had lost her mother—that was negative enough. So I did not need to add any negativity to my life. What I needed to add was positive. So I made it my policy not to watch sad or negative movies, sad or negative television, sad or negative news stories, because I know the damage they can cause. I have always been a fan of watching movies and had always wanted to see the movie *The Green Mile*—a movie that is very well regarded critically. I did not do my research very well and rented it to watch at home. Unfortunately, it was very dark, depressing, and sad. I had to turn the movie off when it was only halfway over. I just couldn't take it. My daughter was very good about warning me about movies that were out in the marketplace that were about a man losing his wife or wife losing her husband, so that I could avoid them. Just to be clear, I'm not talking about avoiding reality. I knew what my reality was—I was a widower. The last thing that I wanted to do was expose myself to death, destruction, disaster, and depression. It can be a downer!

Not only did I make a commitment to avoid negative content, I also made it a point to expose myself to more positive content. Every morning I would get up and have breakfast at the dining room table. While I was eating breakfast, I would select some positive thinking book by one of the great masters like Norman Vincent Peale or Napoleon Hill. I found starting my day with uplifting positive content was a great way to start. I have a fairly large collection of motivational and inspirational books, so my reading assignments were easy to fulfill.

I also was very much focused on not associating with negative people who had negative things to say. I didn't have room for them before in my life, and after I experienced my loss, I found that I had even less room for them.

So there you go—my hope is that by applying these ideas and techniques you can move closer to healing and living life again.

> I believe that you control your destiny, that you can be what you want to be. You can also stop and say, "No, I won't do it, I won't behave this way anymore. I'm lonely and I need people around me, maybe I have to change my methods of behaving," and then you do it.
>
> —LEO BUSCAGLIA

CHAPTER 5

MAKING DIFFICULT DECISIONS EVERY DAY

*"When someone you love dies, and you're not
expecting it, you don't lose her all at once; you lose
her in pieces over a long time—the way the mail
stops coming, and her scent fades from the pillows
and even from the clothes in her closet and drawers.
Gradually, you accumulate the parts of her that
are gone. Just when the day comes—when there's a
particular missing part that overwhelms you with
the feeling that she's gone, forever—there comes
another day, and another specifically missing part."*
—JOHN IRVING, *A Prayer for Owen Meany*

As I MENTIONED IN A PREVIOUS CHAPTER, THERE WILL BE many major and minor decisions to make as a result of your loss. In the early days you'll have to make decisions about funerals, memorial services, burial, cremation, and other logistics relating to funeral services and memorials and headstones. You may have to make these decisions alone, or you may be making these decisions with other family members and close friends; the choice is up to you. The hard part about the entire process is that once the funeral is over, you haven't finished—you have just begun. You will have many tough decisions to make over the next few years. Some of those decisions you will have to make because you will be forced to; some of those decisions will be optional. My hope in this chapter is to give you some valuable tools and techniques to analyze and think through the massive number of difficult decisions you will need to be making. It's not going to be easy, but you can get through it—I promise and I know. I lived them.

There are actually several areas of your life and your family's life you may need to make decisions about:

- Personal items
- Finances/bill paying
- Real estate
- Family and children
- Household management/maintenance
- Timing of decisions
- Work life/career
- Legal matters/wills

THE STUFF THEY LEFT BEHIND

One of the most challenging aspects of grieving a loss, particularly when we are talking about adults, is all of the stuff that they leave behind. Their loved ones have to handle, sort, organize, and make decisions about this stuff. What to do with it all? It also can be extremely painful emotionally because the items that they leave behind are achingly personal. I will never forget the experience of going through my wife's walk-in closet and handling all of her clothes. As I removed clothes from the closet each outfit often brought up a special memory of a specific time and place when she wore that particular outfit, and the calendar of my life with her was flipped back to another page. I could actually see her wearing some of the outfits, or remembered where she bought them. I have to say that was very difficult and painful.

So my friend, one of the biggest questions that you'll have is—what to do with all of "the stuff" (a technical term). From a practical viewpoint, a lot of the items that my wife left behind were things that I had no use for, such as women's clothing and women's perfumes, lotions, makeup, and jewelry. The best advice that I can give you is the technique of "divide and conquer." I also recommend that you ask for help if you feel that you need it. My wife, for example, was a huge fan of what I lovingly call "lotions and potions." Her bathroom was stocked with a huge inventory of lotions, perfumes, and other ladies' cosmetics (OK, maybe too many—but I am glad they made her happy). I asked my daughter if she would come over and help me sort through them and determine first which ones she wanted, which ones might be given to other friends and family members, and which ones we could donate to a good cause. Her assistance in sorting through all of the items in the bathroom was invaluable to me at that time. Besides, as a man what do I know about ladies' cosmetics? But I think her assistance was more than just the expertise about women's cosmetics. She and her husband came over and spent an entire day working with me sorting through all of those items. It was hard for them too, but the moral support I got was extremely helpful that day and made me able to get through a very difficult task that I had to do (one of many on my long road).

So when thinking about the stuff that your loved one left behind, I think you can break it into different categories and decide which you're going to do in what order. For example, after my wife passed away, there were several categories of items that were left behind that needed to be sorted through. They were as follows:

- Clothing
- Cosmetics
- Collectibles
- Books
- Keepsakes
- Photographs
- Computers and technology
- Jewelry
- A truck (as second vehicle—I already had a car)
- An art studio

My wife was a collector and really enjoyed life, so she also had a large number of each of these items. So I started out first with sorting through the makeup and perfumes. I chose this as my best first place to start.

The one thing I want you to think about as you go through this painful and difficult process is that you will have to decide what you are going to do with everything you sort through. Will you give these items to family members? Will you give them to friends? Donate them to charity? Sell them? Will you throw them in the trash? Keep in mind there are no right or wrong answers—all of those decisions are up to you or family members whom you designate and trust.

I was very fortunate to discover that an assistant at my doctor's office was involved with a local charity that helps underprivileged women who were looking for work to become productive members of society. So this charity needed donations of women's clothing and other items. One day when visiting my doctor's office, I was telling her that I was in the process of cleaning out some of Cindy's things. She asked me what items I was cleaning out and I told her about the makeup, perfume, and clothing. As it turns out, this charity needed all of those items for the women who were interviewing for jobs. I was able to donate all of Cindy's clothes and a good portion of her makeup and perfume (that my daughter did not want) to the charity. As for me, it made me feel good that some of Cindy's things were helping another human being on the planet to be successful. For me that was a great legacy for her; it really warmed my heart to know that. They took all of Cindy's unused makeup and subdivided them into small Ziploc bags, and they said that over 60 women received makeup to help them look great on their upcoming job interviews. That was a great feeling. So that helped take care of both the clothing and the makeup and perfume.

The next item I decided to tackle was the jewelry. My wife was a big fan of jewelry. I used a similar process in sorting through all of the jewelry by asking my daughter and her husband to help me. She determined what she wanted to take; I determined which pieces I wanted to keep—ones that had sentimental value—and which ones to give away to friends and family. I also decided to sell some of the gold and silver jewelry, because as a practical matter, it was just too much to keep.

It has been 22 months and I have taken care of most of the items on the list. I'm still working through some of the items such as the collectibles and the art studio. Here are some of the questions that I ask myself which seem helpful in deciding how to sort through things.

- Does this item have sentimental value to me or someone else in the family?
- Is this an item that I want to keep for myself?
- Is this an item I want to give away?
- If I give this item away, who do I want to give it to?
- Is it an item I could sell?
- If I donated it, who would it be donated to?
- Is it OK to throw this item away?

Let me also address a fairly obvious issue. I am sure there will be some people reading this book who are offended when I talk about throwing things away. I'm not talking about throwing away family heirlooms or things that have tremendous sentimental value. I found for me there was an overwhelming number of items to go through. I determined the items that could be given to other people—friends and family. If an item had no other value and could not be donated to charity then I threw it away. My thinking was that there's only so much time in a day and being incredibly busy (doing all of the things that two people used to do), I had to get practical and realize that there were some things that just belonged in the trash. That was not meant as an act of disrespect toward my late wife, they were just things that I did not need, no one else wanted, or could not be donated.

The reason I bring this up is, even though you are grieving, it still is a good idea to be practical. After all, how much can you reasonably expect to keep? To me the key rule in sorting through things is to not be impractical, while at the same time making sure that you make decisions that you're comfortable with. I got rid of my wife's clothes about four months after she died. Some people would say that's too soon, some people would say that's not soon enough. The reality is it doesn't matter what people say, what matters is what is right for you. Please don't feel rushed or pressured to do it sooner or to do it later. Do what feels right for you. I will say this: when you clean up, reorganize, and get rid of things, it can make you feel like you are moving forward in a positive way. I think it is good for your healing.

THE MONEY

It's a harsh, cold reality of life that not long after your loss you will be forced to take a look at all things financial, otherwise you are going to have more issues. It is the worst time to have to do these tasks because you are emotionally distraught, and it's very hard to think clearly. I can tell you truthfully I found it agonizing. However, if you do not take a look at the financial picture, it will cause you even more suffering. If you are in a relationship and you were the one who handled the finances, it will not be as difficult. In our marriage my wife was the bill payer, and she handled all of those responsibilities. My challenge was to immediately take over the bill-paying function because bills had to be paid. I mean—I do have a mortgage payment and I kind of like my house. An additional challenge was that I was not allowed access to our bank's online bill payment, so I had to dig through piles of mail to determine who we paid bills to and when each of them were due. I also had to research all of the account numbers and information. This took a great deal of time.

My only warning is to look at this sooner rather than later, because even with the loss, companies are not empathetic and most will not allow you to miss a payment. This could affect your credit negatively in the future. In addition to paying bills, there will be several other areas that you will need to address. I know that I didn't want to address any of this—and I know you probably do not want to either—but painful as it may be, life must go on, and particularly your financial life carries on every month. Some of the questions you may ask yourself about finances are:

- How many bank accounts are there and how much money is in each one?

- Do you have the passwords and access information to look at each of them online or in person?

- Is there a safety deposit box with valuables and do you have the key?

- Are there any active life insurance policies in place that require action for payout?

- Can you still afford to live in your house or apartment now that the loved one's income has gone away?

- Do you have outstanding loans or mortgage payments that will be difficult to pay on just your income?

- Do you have a household financial budget for the month? Does it need to be reworked due to the changes that have happened?

- How many vehicles do you want to keep and are they paid off?

So those are just a few questions you might want to think through regarding money and finances.

REAL ESTATE

When my wife passed away I lived in a 2,800 square foot Cape Cod house on 1.7 acres. For months after my wife passed away I was asked, "What are you going to do with the house?" My answer was always the same: "I don't know." It was too big of a house for one man and four cats—and it was very lonely and empty. I made up my mind that I was not going to make any major decisions on the house until I was ready; I was very fortunate that I wasn't going to be forced financially to make a decision. I was OK there.

So my point is you do need to take a look at your housing situation and look at it from a financial and emotional perspective. So financially, can you make your house payment on one income (if your loss eliminated an income producer)? If not, what can you do? Can you get a roommate? If you live in an apartment the same questions apply.

Next—what about the emotional component of where you live? The house I live in is also the house where my wife passed away. Some people would not be able to live in a house where their wife died. Perhaps I'm too practical, but I don't blame the house and it doesn't bother me that she passed away here. It was her home, our home for sixteen years. It feels like home to me. However, you may have certain emotional feelings about your house or your apartment that are too hard for you to overcome. My only advice would be not to make decisions immediately because your feelings may change long term, and I don't want you to make a financial mistake by selling too quickly and by making rash decisions that are not financially sound. In the long run, it is really, totally your decision as to whether you want to stay in the home you're living in or if you want to live somewhere different. The choice is yours.

FAMILY AND CHILDREN

I was very fortunate to have grown children and no young children when my wife passed away. I have one daughter who at the time of the writing of this book is 28 years old. She is married and has a happy life with her husband. I do know that when people have a loss of a husband or a wife there is a great deal of complexity that is added when they have young children as well. First, the husband or wife is experiencing the loss of their spouse, and then they are also suffering through the pain that their children are feeling because they lost their mother or father. This is compounded when the children are a young age and don't really understand the concept of death and can't figure out where Mommy or Daddy went. There is no doubt that when someone suffers a loss, the dynamics of the family are affected in every way you can imagine.

So you will be facing a whole range of issues relating to family and children as result of your loss. There will be all sorts of complicated issues that will come up, and you will need to be strong and thoughtful in handling each and every situation in the family that will develop. People will be looking to you for the answers.

I remember going to my mom and dad's house for Christmas about seven months after my wife passed away. I felt entirely at ease and comfortable, but I think there were people in the family who worried that I would not feel comfortable on Christmas Day or that I would be feeling melancholy because I was celebrating Christmas without my wife. I was actually OK. So the dynamic for me changed, but I didn't realize that the dynamic for everyone else changed around me as well. That is the overwhelming effect of grief. It is like a ripple in a pond—we drop the stone of death in the middle and grief creates ripples which go outward and affect everybody in the water. I think you can ask yourself some primary questions which you will find helpful when making decisions about family and children:

1. What is the best solution for me at this time being a person in grief?

2. What is the best solution for the children at this time—being that they are children in grief?

3. What are the best solutions for other family members at this time relating to family and children?

There is a rank order to these questions and that is very deliberate. Some would say that I should be asking the question about what's best for the children first—I passionately disagree. I think you have to ask what is best for you first because you are the one who will be raising or dealing with the children from this point forward. You are the primary caregiver—you must take care of yourself first and the children second. If you don't take care of yourself, you will not be able to help your children. I also would highly recommend, if needed, to consult with a mental health professional to get their advice on what would be best for both you and the children.

HOUSEHOLD MANAGEMENT AND MAINTENANCE

Once my wife passed away I realized that I was now faced with a huge challenge. Simply put—I was now responsible for doing everything. My wife did not work outside of the home so she took care of bill paying, shopping for groceries, and many other household duties. So I now realized that I had to take care of getting the house clean, shopping for groceries, laundry, paying the bills, and taking care of four cats. That was in addition to running a business and traveling on business frequently. I immediately felt somewhat overwhelmed by all of my new responsibilities while grieving at the same time.

So my advice would be to take a hard look at your list of responsibilities and determine how you're going to handle them short term and midterm. I cleaned the house for the first two to three months and then determined it was just taking up too much of my time and energy, so I hired a housecleaning service. I was very fortunate to be in a financial position where I could comfortably afford to hire them. Because of my frequent business travel, I also decided to hire a pet sitter to come to the house and feed my cats when I was out of town. It was either that or get rid of the cats, and I just couldn't do that.

So in looking at your new responsibilities, consider who is going to handle the following items:

- bill paying
- laundry
- grocery shopping
- housecleaning
- lawn care
- child care
- household maintenance
- car maintenance and inspection

Those are just a few of the items you may want to take a look at. Don't hesitate to ask people for help in the early days if you need assistance. Just know that eventually you're going to need to take on the responsibilities yourself or hire people to do them for you. Unfortunately, the way life is set up, these are not items that you can skip or not take care of; and in fact if you neglect them they'll end up costing you a lot of money, time, and effort later on.

TIMING OF DECISIONS

In terms of making decisions about everything in your life, I cannot tell you when the right time or the wrong time is to make them. Certainly, you do not want to make decisions when you're too emotional to be thinking clearly, but on the other hand, sometimes you don't want to delay decisions for too long because that might be detrimental for you.

I have three pieces of advice for making decisions when you are grieving a loss.

First: listen to your heart. I often think in our society that people don't rely enough on their instincts. Often you'll already know the right answer, if you're just listening to your own internal voice talk. If something feels right and you have given it enough time and thought (as judged by you), then go ahead and do it. Don't second-guess yourself and realize that you really are doing the very best you can under trying and difficult circumstances.

Second: tap in to your team of advisors. I highly recommend having a team of trusted advisors who can give you sound advice and wisdom during your time of loss. Make sure that these are people who are positive and optimistic and have your best interests at heart. I surrounded myself with a team of very wise advisors who helped me greatly during my most difficult days. I had my best friend, his wife, my buddy Joe, my uncle, and my brother, sister, and my parents. The other advantage you have in having a team of advisors is they can be objective about your situation. If you are faced with legal or financial situations, seek out professionals in those fields.

Third: read and study. If you're trying to make decisions about important life situations, try to find good books on the topic that would help you. Sometimes we try to figure things out on our own; however, I believe when grieving a loss it is a good idea to tap in to other people's expertise.

WORK LIFE AND CAREER

I am a professional speaker and book author. After my wife passed away, there were some people who asked me what I intended to do in terms of my career as a result of my loss. I said without hesitating that I would not stop speaking or training or consulting because this is the work that I love doing, this is the work that I have a passion for, and I don't know why I would stop doing it. However, I do believe sometimes there are life circumstances that people face as a result of the loss that may force them to make a change, or they may choose to make changes in what they do for a living. I cannot tell you what the right answer is for you. If you are a truck driver, for example, and are always out on the road and your partner or spouse stayed home taking care of your children, then maybe if you lost your spouse you would have to stop being a long-haul truck driver to be home with your children. I would encourage you to take a long hard look at your profession and determine if you need to make any modifications or changes as a result of the loss of a loved one.

LEGAL MATTERS AND WILLS

I have been involved with circumstances in the past where families were split apart because of wills, legal matters, and inheritances. Your first step is to find out if the person you lost had a will, where that will is located, and who the executor of the will is. The next step would be getting involved with an attorney to determine the proper steps for handling the legal matters relating to the loss of a loved one. In my opinion, one of the most devastating situations that you can get involved with after the loss of a loved one is disputes, arguments, and fights over what people inherit, or with what the will says. If I were you I would make a very deliberate decision not to get emotionally involved with those issues. Family drama and arguments are not what you need in your life right now. They will just add to your level of stress.

So those are some of the key areas you'll need to make decisions on. Just point your compass in a direction, navigate, and do the best you can. That really is all you can do, right?

To close this chapter—I think Shel Silverstein said it best about making decisions:

THE VOICE

There is a voice inside of you
That whispers all day long,
"I feel this is right for me,
I know that this is wrong."
No teacher, preacher, parent, friend
Or wise man can decide
What's right for you—just listen to
The voice that speaks inside.
—SHEL SILVERSTEIN

CHAPTER 6

HOW GRIEF CAN GET TO YOU: POSSIBLE RESPONSES TO GRIEF

"It is a curious thing, the death of a loved one. We all
know that our time in this world is limited, and that
eventually all of us will end up underneath some sheet,
never to wake up. And yet it is always a surprise when
it happens to someone we know. It is like walking up the
stairs to your bedroom in the dark, and thinking there is
one more stair than there is. Your foot falls down, through
the air, and there is a sickly moment of dark surprise as
you try and readjust the way you thought of things."
—LEMONY SNICKET, *Horseradish:*
Bitter Truths You Can't Avoid

YEARS AGO THERE WAS VERY POPULAR BOOK OUT FOR PREGnant women called *What to Expect When You Are Expecting*. I thought that it was a brilliant book because it let pregnant women know what they could expect each month of their pregnancy. I also thought it was a good idea, because it helped both the husband and the wife know what to expect during nine months of pregnancy. My hope is in this chapter I can also help you understand what may possibly be your responses to grief. As much as you are grieving, I want you to be aware of the emotions and feelings you're having, but I also want you to know that you're not alone. Many of us grieving people have experienced the same things. Awareness and knowledge is half the battle for overcoming anxiety. So I've outlined for you several possible reactions to grief and how you can handle each one of them, should they happen to be the ones that you're experiencing.

BEING NUMB

It is quite possible after the experience of losing a loved one you may just feel like you are in shock. Well, you are in shock. You may not have very many emotions. In fact, you may feel numb, not feeling too high or too low—just numb. If this is the case with you—don't worry. Eventually you will stop being numb and you will start to feel. The challenge is when you start to feel the emotions of sadness, grief, and loss, and also some positive emotions as well. Just know that those are completely normal emotions and it's OK to allow the process in your grief because you need to get it out of your system so you can start to feel again.

ANGER

There's absolutely no question that anger is a normal human reaction to grief. You may be angry that your loved one died. You may be angry that life was cut short. You may be furious that it happened to you and your family. I mean, after all, why you, why your loved one, why your family? Did you win some sort of strange death lottery? It just seems so very unfair.

I did experience times when I was feeling angry and frustrated, particularly when sorting through paying bills or cleaning up a very messy room. My advice about the anger is that it is OK to vent, and in fact you have to vent in order to dissipate your anger. It is not good for your health to keep it bottled up inside you. So express your anger by yelling, screaming, or crying, and after that you will feel better. Punch a pillow. Just make sure when you're expressing your anger to do it in the right place— privately, so that you will not unduly concern other people.

It is also perfectly acceptable to express your anger if you're around someone you love and trust who will not judge you or get upset that you're angry, someone who understands your pain. I also found that physical activity was a big help in over- coming the frustration of anger. Working out helped to burn off the steam. If you feel like the anger is unmanageable, then seek out help from a mental health professional or a counselor. It amazes me in this country that there still is sometimes a stigma about seeking help from a mental health professional. We all go to the doctor for a broken arm but hesitate to seek out help when we have emotional issues. Don't hesitate—if you feel like you need the help, then go find it.

DISTRACTION

You may find that your grief causes you to be mas- sively distracted both at work and at home. This is very understandable as you've been through a devastating expe-rence. It's not easy to focus on life when some major event in your life has changed everything and shattered the glass of your former life. I found in the first couple of months it was really hard for me to focus on my work, but I knew that I had to buckle down and concentrate because I did not want to create any issues with my business, which I knew would cause me more stress. Something I found to be helpful in keeping me focused was to daily make a specific list of things I needed to get done, both personally and profession-ally. I would then refer back to the list several times a day to keep myself on track. I also think it's not a bad idea to take breaks every few hours so that you don't have to focus quite as long, and your brain will be more refreshed after you've taken a short break.

NIGHTMARES

Every day while you are grieving, your conscious mind is dealing with your loss in several ways. However, your subcon-scious mind is also wrestling with grief even though you're not aware of it. Your subconscious mind is on autopilot 24/7 trying to figure out and process the loss that has happened. My theory is that the nightmares that come about while you are asleep are your subconscious mind "acting out" what it has been processing all day. It may be processing guilt or anger or confusion or frustration or shock. I wish I never had night-mares, but god, I did. I eventually started dating again after my wife passed away. About two weeks after I started dating, I started having a horrible nightmare over and over. There would be a knock on my front door, and when I opened the door my late wife was standing there smiling, and she said, "Hi honey, I am back!" and gave me a big hug. In my nightmare, I am delighted to have her back, but immediately I'm overcome with terrible guilt, because I have already been dating someone else. I then have to tell her that I am dating someone else, and she is of course emotionally devastated because she felt like I was "cheating" on her.

I was married and faithful to my vows for 32 years, so any cheating accusation would be devastating for me. I then have to justify and explain why I started dating and how it was not meant as a slight to her. You can imagine how painful the conversation in my nightmare was. Everything in the nightmare seemed so very real, like watching a movie in my head, and I would then wake up in my bed in a cold sweat realizing that it was all just a nightmare! Let me tell you that nightmare really hurt, because I never would want to hurt my late wife's feelings and the nightmare was so traumatic. My subconscious mind was all worked up.

I also had several other horrific nightmares—I won't go into the details—that were difficult to deal with emotionally. So how do you overcome nightmares? The bad news is I had the same nightmare many times; the good news is it eventually stopped. So if you have nightmares, shake them off, move forward, and they will eventually stop. I also added an additional routine at bedtime which seemed to help (you may want to try this too). My routine was that I would make sure to think positive thoughts right before I went to sleep, and that seemed to help as well.

BEING IMPULSIVE

When we experience grief, sometimes a solution for getting out of the grief is to do impulsive things to help us feel better. It's almost like going through a midlife crisis, even though you may not be in midlife. I thought about taking a trip to Paris; I thought about buying a new car; I thought about collecting art. I thought about, believe it or not, getting a facelift because I was not happy with my appearance at the time and saw an ad on television for Lifestyle Lift. I went to their offices and met with them and talked to the consultant, and then all the way home said to myself, "Am I doing this because I need plastic surgery, or am I doing this just because I'm trying to feel better?" I decided not to.

I saw an ad for Cenegenics (a company specializing in age management and hormone replacement therapy). They specialize in hormone replacement for men and women over 50 years old. They have an ad where a 60-year-old man has a 60-year-old face but has a body that looks like he is 35. They use nutrition, diet, and growth hormones to get amazing results. I had a long discussion with one of their associates. When I realized that it was going to cost me $12,000 a year I decided to not pursue that either.

At the time all of these things that I was doing seemed to be logical and thoughtful. As I look back on it now, I kind of chuckle to myself. I was actually being impulsive and trying to find some way to make myself feel better. In the early days of your grief process, just be aware that you may end up being a bit too impulsive. The solution to this is just to make sure to think about and evaluate everything that you're doing. Do not rush into doing anything big.

THE SPECIAL DAY BLUES

Many people who have had a loss experience what I call the "special day blues." On any special day (like a holiday) or a wedding anniversary, the birthday of the person who passed away, or the anniversary day of their death, it can be tough to deal with. For example, my calendar will always have May 4th circled because that is the day that my wife passed. I will never have a May 4 go by when I will not think of what happened on that very day. I have two pieces of advice.

1. You may decide to commemorate those special days by getting together with friends and family to remember the person who passed away in either a formal service such as a ceremony or just a get-together.

2. You may also decide that you don't want to get together with other people and just want to remember the day quietly on your own.

When we approached the one-year anniversary of my wife's death, I called my daughter and asked her how she wanted to handle that day. She decided rather than getting together that she would prefer to quietly remember her mom on that day with her and her husband alone at home. I was glad she said that because I felt pretty much the same way. There is no right or a wrong answer in this equation. It is solely up to you to decide what works for you. I think people also struggle with their loved ones not being with them around Christmas and New Year's and other holidays like Thanksgiving. The first ones are always the toughest, but I can only tell you that with each holiday that goes by, it does get easier.

JEALOUSY

It seems odd to mention jealousy in a book about grief. But I can tell you (I am embarrassed to admit it but I will), I was painfully aware that I was being jealous and was experiencing the strong emotion of jealousy. I travel often as a professional speaker, and often while sitting in airports across America I would see a happy, loving couple who was about my age. The couples I would see were boyfriend and girlfriend or husband and wife. I could see them laughing and flirting and having a good time, and I was insanely jealous. Why did this man still have his wife and I did not? Why was I denied? So I would sit watching the happy couple and feeling angry that they had what I no longer had. But I knew that jealousy is a very destructive emotion and only hurts you and those around you. My advice for handling jealousy is to focus on the future. I would say to myself, "Yes, you do not have a loved one now to share your life with, but you will in the future." I would also say to myself that I was happy that they had someone to share their life with, and to focus on being happy for them.

FEELING LIKE LIFE IS PILING ON

I will admit that there were times in the first couple of months after my wife passed away that I felt like life was picking on me and piling on. Sometimes I'd say to myself, "Gee, life—is there anything else you'd like to throw at me?" In a several month time frame, I lost my wife, one of my cats died, I had to take over all of the bill paying and take over all of the housework, had to find a pet sitter for my cats, and the list went on. There were a few days when I sat with my head in my hands because my patience was being tried to the max. My advice, if you feel like life is piling on, is to find trusted friends you can talk to in order to vent, and to seek advice. I found my support system to be a tremendous help when I was feeling like life was piling on. Second, you can also think, "This too will pass," meaning you will eventually get through it all and things will get better. Lastly, life is really not piling on—it just happens to feel that way, and sometimes people are put in unfortunate situations that don't seem fair at all, but they are what they are. Keep pushing forward.

LACK OF DIRECTION

Sometimes when we have a significant loss in our life it is hard for us to think about what is going to be next. When my wife passed away, all of the goals and dreams that we had as a couple were immediately destroyed. Yes, I had goals for myself personally and professionally, but my identity was firmly wrapped around being a married person. Suddenly I was a single person and no longer part of the couple. So many integral parts of my life were suddenly changed. This can lead to feeling like there is no direction in your life, and in some ways that is probably true because you have to recalculate where you're going. Chapter 9 is an entire chapter to help you navigate your future and decide where it is you want to go.

LACK OF OPTIMISM

When we lose a father, mother, spouse, or child, it is very easy to say to ourselves, "What the heck is there to be optimistic about?" That is certainly a very legitimate question, and I can understand why many people feel that way. I have always lived my life as an optimist; I always think that things will go well and things will get better. Even after the devastating loss of my wife, I always knew in my heart that eventually I would live a happy life again.

So how do you regain your optimism? As mentioned briefly in Chapter 3, one of the things that can help us is to make what I call a gratitude list. This is simply a list of all of the things that you are grateful for that you have in your life. For example, if I am making my gratitude list I could say the following: I am grateful that I am alive, that I have my health, that I have a lovely house, that I do not have financial difficulties, that I own my own company, that I love the work that I do, that I have a wonderful daughter and son-in-law, I have wonderful parents who are healthy and in their 80s, I am close to my brother and sister, and I have three mischievous, wonderful cats. Sit down with a pad of paper and write down all of the things that you are grateful for. Sometimes, when we realize that even though we have had a loss there's still a lot that we do have, we can regain some sense of optimism. Another way to improve your level of optimism is to read books about positive thinking and how to think more optimistically. Trust me, this is something that you can regain.

TROUBLE AT WORK

I know after you have had a devastating loss it is really tough to go back to work. They gave you some time off to recover from your grief, but it was not nearly long enough. So now you go back to the workplace with people who have normal lives and have not had the loss that you have had. This can be very difficult and awkward. It is often very hard to concentrate and to get your work done at the same performance level as before you had your loss. But I will tell you this, and I am going to be blunt: you have to perform at work, because if you don't they will let you go. If you get fired then your problems will be multiplied, because you will be grieving and unemployed. You do not need the additional stress and anxiety of being unemployed while you are grieving. So my advice is to put on your suit of armor and to go in to work with the determination to stay focused for those eight hours. When you go home, you can fall apart and grieve and cry, but nope—not at work. The only way I know how to describe it is that you have to learn how to fake it (that you are calm, cool, and collected even when you're not), because the workplace will not give you enough time to grieve. So you have to give the illusion that you have recovered and you can handle it. Suck it up and learn how to be focused while you are at work.

ALCOHOL AND DRUGS

A terrible idea that I guarantee will make your grief worse, not better. Avoid it. It will just hide the pain, not take it away. No one feels better by drinking—only worse.

TOO MUCH TV

Just like alcohol and drugs, TV can be a convenient escape from the real world, and it can be a form of anesthesia. There are three issues about TV. One, TV can suck you in to watching hours of meaningless TV and waste an entire evening or day. Two, most TV is extremely negative, and as I've mentioned in another chapter, you need to avoid exposing yourself to negative content and material. The last issue is that TV can cause you to be extremely antisocial because you're not getting out and being around people—just sitting in your house watching TV in the dark. So I suggest really being aware of how much TV you watch a week and limiting the amount of time you do. Instead, find activities that get you more involved with human beings.

OVERWHELMED

I know of parents who have lost a spouse. They then have the double duty of not only grieving the loss of their husband or wife, but they still have children to take care of. One of the biggest emotions that I see with some people who are grieving is they do feel overwhelmed, not only by their grief but by the enormous responsibilities they now face. I was fortunate that there was no child living at home when my wife passed away. So I did not have the responsibility of caring for children. However, I did feel somewhat overwhelmed because I did have to run a business, run a household, and do all of the things that two people used to do. Suddenly everything was on my shoulders and there were days when I felt quite overwhelmed.

So how do you overcome the feeling of being overwhelmed? I think it's OK to ask friends and family for help when you feel that you really need it. Also understand that you can only do so much in one day. You are one person. Make a list of things that you need to get done and do the best you can. Some things may have to wait until tomorrow, and you have to decide in advance that it's OK. The good news is that once you start to get down your routines and your processes, you will get better at doing all of those things and you will start to feel less overwhelmed. If you do have children at home, you may need to assign them additional responsibilities to take some of the pressure off of you. They will probably want to help and make their contribution to the family.

PHYSICAL LACK OF CARING

When you are in the early days of the grieving process, you may not feel like taking such good care of yourself. You may not want to eat, you may not want to sleep, and you may not want to take a shower. I understand; I was there. In Chapter 7, I cover how to take good care of yourself so that you can take good care of others. What I found was when I did take a shower and shave and get dressed, I felt better about myself.

DEPRESSION

I was very fortunate because even though I was sad during the first several months of my grief process I never felt as if I was depressed. If you are depressed as a result of your loss, it is certainly very understandable. To me the key is how depressed you are and for how long. If you are depressed for a short amount of time, I don't think that is an issue; in fact, it's probably a normal reaction. However, if you are depressed for an extended period of time, I strongly urge you to seek out counseling from a mental health professional or join a grief support group. A mental health professional will be able to help you talk through your depression and may even be able to prescribe some antidepressants to help you get through your healing process. A grief support group gives you the ability to talk about what happened and how you feel about your loss with other people who have had similar losses.

AWKWARDNESS

I found that losing my wife and going from being married to single was a very awkward feeling. I even commented to friends and family during the first week that I could not believe that I was single. I also found that meeting people out in public often became a very awkward conversation, because they would ask about my wife and I would then have to explain that I was a widower. This conversation then became a burden for me and for the person I was speaking with. How do you deal with awkwardness? The answer is you really just have to push through it, and eventually you will feel more comfortable with telling people that you are a widower or you lost a child or you lost a parent or friend. The awkwardness over time just goes away.

APATHY

I think many people grieving a loss sometimes go into a phase of apathy, and they really don't care too much about what happens in their life. I was very fortunate that I did not experience the emotion of apathy. But I have seen and talked to many people who were in an apathetic state and became very disconnected from things that happened in their life. I also believe that time will pull people out of their apathy as they begin to heal. If the condition of apathy continues for an extended time, it's a good idea to seek out counseling help. You want to live a life where you actually care about what you're doing, the people you are with, and for the people who love you. Caring and loving is part of living.

BEING ANTISOCIAL

Sitting in your house day after day and not getting out to be with people is a very bad idea. I found for me that if I sat around my house too long, I began dwelling on things that for me had no inherent value. Let me explain what I mean. I could sit and grieve for two hours, or I could sit and grieve for four hours. In my opinion two hours was plenty and four hours was just not good for me. So being antisocial and not being around people actually makes you feel sadder—not less sad. It just reminds you more about being alone. So really make an effort to get out and do something and don't be anti-social. I believe that human beings are not meant to be alone but are meant to be around other human beings. Please don't misunderstand; it's OK to be alone at times to think through your life and what has happened. But I don't believe that it is natural or normal to isolate yourself and not interact with others.

PERSONALITY CHANGES

You may find that certain parts of your personality may change temporarily as a result of being in grief. If you were once happy-go-lucky, you may be less happy-go-lucky. If you were calm, you may be a little more stressed. Maybe you develop a tendency to get angry quickly. I believe that some personality changes while you are grieving are perfectly normal. After all, you've been through a tough time and it's not surprising that you would be more sensitive or more anxious.

So my suggestion for dealing with personality changes is just to give yourself a break. You have been through a very tough time and I think you need to forgive yourself and not be so hard on yourself if you slip up here or there. I also think that the people around you will understand because they know what you have been going through. The good news is, as you heal your personality will probably go back to something similar to what it was before. Also be aware that there may be some aspects of your personality that will change forever. I have found that there are a few aspects of my personality that have changed and probably will not go back to the way that they were. I am OK with that.

REACTION TO TRIGGERS

What is a trigger? There will be times when you will hear a certain song, smell a certain scent, taste a certain food, or see something in a movie that will immediately and strongly remind you of the one you've lost. I often found that these emotional triggers caught me off-guard. You can't help it—that trigger just immediately reminds you of the other person and makes you sad.

I recently went into my local convenience store to pick up a few things. As I walked through the back of the store, I noticed the coffee section and smelled a certain coffee blend which was the one that my wife used to always drink. It immediately reminded me of her and made me a little bit sad. People who have not gone through the grief process will never understand what I mean, but you have, you get it. While we can't control our triggers to things in life that we experience, we can control our reaction to the triggers if we are in a public place. The good news is as your time of grief gets longer, the triggers will be less severe and your reaction to them will be more subtle.

So those are just some of the things you may experience in your reactions to grief. Just know you are not alone, you are not a freak or a weirdo—you're just a person like me who is hurting and trying real hard to get through one of life's most difficult and heart-crushing times. It's a tough journey, but you can get through it.

To be hopeful in bad times is not just foolishly romantic. It is based on the fact that human history is a history not only of cruelty, but also of compassion, sacrifice, courage, kindness.

What we choose to emphasize in this complex history will determine our lives. If we see only the worst, it destroys our capacity to do something. If we remember those times and places—and there are so many—where people have behaved magnificently, this gives us the energy to act, and at least the possibility of sending this spinning top of a world in a different direction.

And if we do act, in however small a way, we don't have to wait for some grand utopian future. The future is an infinite succession of presents, and to live now as we think human beings should live, in defiance of all that is bad around us, is itself a marvelous victory.

—HOWARD ZINN

CHAPTER 7

THE RULES YOU MUST FOLLOW: (NOT!)

"There is a club in this world that you do not join knowingly. One day you are just a member. It is 'The life changing events club.' The fee to join the club is hurt beyond belief, payable in full, up front for a lifetime membership. The benefit of the club is a newfound perspective on life, and a deep understanding that you may not be happy about your current situation, but you can be happy in your current situation. The only rule to the club is that you cannot tell anyone that you are a member. The club does not provide a directory of its members, but when you look into a member's eye, you can tell that they too are part of the club. Members are allowed to exchange that brief eye contact that says: 'I didn't know.' Being a member of this club is the last thing that anyone initially wants in their life. Being a member of this club is the best thing that ever happens to a person in their life, and there is not a person in the club that would ever give up their membership. If you really look and know what you are looking for, you can spot the club's members; they are the ones that provide a random act of kindness

and do something for someone who can never repay
them for what they have done. They are the people
spreading joy and optimism and lifting people's spirits
even when their own heart has been broken. I have
paid my dues; my lifetime membership arrived today,
not by mail, but by a deep inner feeling that I cannot
describe. It is the best club that I never wanted to
be part of. But I am glad that I am a member."
—JOHN PASSARO, *6 Minutes Wrestling With Life*

I COVERED IN ANOTHER CHAPTER THE MANY MYTHS AND misinformation people have about grief. In this chapter I wanted to share with you society's rules about grief and what you can do to navigate around them. Yes, I know you already have enough stress and pressure dealing with grief, and now you have to deal with other people's perceptions of what the rules are relating to grief. Why does our society have so many preconceived notions about the rules? My guess is that people are ill-informed about death and are passing along what they have heard during their life as the rules. The reality is there are none. So I want you to continually think about the fact that there are no rules for how you handle grief. It is up to you to decide how you handle every aspect of your life. So here are 12 rules you can expect people to try to hold you to even though none of them are actually true.

Rule #1: There are rules.

Somehow our society made determinations about exactly how a grieving person should conduct themselves at all times.

If we expected other people to live by our pre-defined rules, they would actually resent it. Yet for some strange reason it seems perfectly OK to tell a grieving person how to live. *Hmm.* One of the things that I find fascinating is that people often don't realize they are dictating the rules—they're just blindly following social "norms."

The problem is—what is normal? Your loved one dying was not normal. Your loved one passing away tragically was not normal. Your loved one dying too young was not normal. Your loved one dying before her parents was not normal. Your loved one being killed in a tragic accident was not normal. So my point is that none of this is truly normal. It's all, well— just weird, and sometimes very surreal, like we are caught in a real-life nightmare. So I don't know why people are trying to dictate norms for something that's not normal! So I want you to constantly keep this in the back of your head: Do what you want with your life and don't let other people tell you what the rules are. Besides, trying to live up to someone else's set of life rules is exhausting and counterproductive, and it will drive you crazy.

Rule breaker solution: My suggestion for you about the rules is to ignore them all, except for rules that make sense to you and feel right. Don't let other people dictate your life to you.

Rule #2: You must act in a certain way.

I don't know what way you're supposed to act, but one of the things that I found fascinating (OK, I admit, I'm a geek about studying human nature) was during the early days of my grief, people were constantly watching *how* I grieved. Oh sure, I know people were worried and concerned about me, which I very much appreciated. But some people said things to me that indicated they were carefully watching how I was grieving. Several people said something like, "You seem to be doing really well," indicating they were almost surprised at how well I was doing. The mistake in their perception was they were only looking at how I was reacting on the outside—not at my internal emotions.

I see people who expect a grieving person to act in a certain way—they should be crying more, should be crying less, should be acting more depressed, less depressed. It's almost as if the person who is in grief has been cast in a role as a grieving brother, father, sister, mother, or spouse, and those roles need to be portrayed in a certain way. The reality is there is no one "right way" to act when you are grieving. I wish people would stop clinging to the stereotype of what a griever looks like and acts like.

Rule breaker solution: My advice to you on this rule is to simply be yourself and don't worry about how you are supposed to or not supposed to act. If people want to misinterpret your actions as being inappropriate then that is their problem. This is you and your family's time—not theirs.

Rule #3: Certain activities are not appropriate for someone who is grieving.

Our society seems to have determined that certain activities are not appropriate for someone who is grieving. Now please don't misunderstand what I'm saying. I'm not saying this idea applies to going to a party three days after losing a loved one. But what I am saying is people certainly judge what activities grieving people should or should not do, and also when they should do them. After my wife passed away, I often felt as if I was being confined in the house, just sitting around staring at the four walls. After a good deal of thought and reflection I realized it was not good for me to stay stagnant. So I started going out to the mall, to art galleries, and to amusement parks. All of these activities were done, yes—by myself. Often my cell phone would ring and the person on the other end would ask me what I was doing. I would tell them that I was shopping, or at an amusement park, or having dinner and getting ready to go to the movies.

In the early days I think people who called me were often surprised that I was out doing something. The loneliness and the isolation of sitting around the house were not good for me—I needed to be out and around other human beings. I also had learned a great lesson about life being too short, and I decided very early in my grief process not to waste a minute. I think this confused some people and in some cases even caused some people to be concerned about me, because they didn't understand why I was doing the things I was doing.

There is even an implication at times that a person who is grieving and engaging in some activity is somehow being disrespectful to the loved one who has gone. This could not be further from the truth, and I find it to be offensive. Just because I was at the movies didn't mean I was grieving any less or that I was not constantly thinking about my loss. On the other hand, I did not think it was good for my health to sit in the house, isolated, staring at the four walls. So for me, going on a hike or going to the gym or going to the mall was very therapeutic. As the person grieving, prepare for people to react to you in odd ways when they think that you're doing activities that are inappropriate for someone who is grieving.

Rule breaker solution: Ignore them. It's their problem, not yours. The bottom line is that it is up to you to decide at this point what is best for you. Listen to your heart and your instincts, they will tell you what feels right and what doesn't. Unfortunately, friends, family, and acquaintances don't necessarily know what's best for you—just what would be "normal" under the circumstances.

Rule #4: There is a right time to wait before dating.

Wrong, wrong, wrong. Nothing is more ridiculous than that statement. As I discussed in an earlier chapter, I decided to start dating about four months after my wife passed away. Please don't pay too much attention to the four months. In my opinion it doesn't matter whether it was four months or four years. There is no right answer because the answer is different for every single person.

I am a very loving person. I am and have always been a people person. As a result of my loss, I felt extremely, devastatingly lonely, walking around an empty house without a loved one. Due to the guidance of my best friend and advice from other valued friends and family, I decided when the right time was for me. I have had many friends and family members tell me stories of people from their church or from their neighborhood who have lost a loved one and have been remarried within one year. They then tell me how scandalized everyone was that this person moved so quickly to "replace" their husband or their wife. This really is such an insult to the person who was in grief. There is no replacing my wife, Cindy. I did not start dating looking for a doppelgänger of my wife with the same looks, hair color, eye color, and personality. No, I was looking for someone to spend my life with, someone to love, someone who shared my values.

Rule breaker solution: My advice on this rule is for you to determine what is right for you. No one else on the planet can tell you how you feel in your heart and your mind about the possibility of dating after you've lost a husband, wife, girlfriend, or boyfriend. They can't see inside of your heart, they can't peer into your soul and know what you feel and believe. They can only go by what you tell them.

If life is short (and anyone who is reading this book knows that it is), then what is the point of waiting to meet some sort of arbitrary rule about time? Are we supposed to wait one year? Are we supposed to wait two years? Are we supposed to wait three years? What if we meet someone and fall in love after waiting for four years? Then we may say to ourselves, "I wish I would've met this person three years ago because I lost years with them." In my opinion it is not disrespectful in any way to the memory of the person you lost. They would want you to go on, and they most certainly would want you to be happy. So don't worry about the people who will be scandalized or upset or frustrated that you have started dating too soon.

Rule breaker solution: Go out into the world of dating and seek joy and love. I also believe that finding joy and love and companionship will help you heal more quickly in the griev-ing process. Once you start dating—then people will also have preconceived notions about what you should and should not be doing. They will say you're dating too soon, you are not dating soon enough, you're dating too many people, and not enough people. Again, all of these decisions are up to you.

Rule #5: They have to give you permission.

I felt, in many cases, as people were talking to me during the early days of my grief process that they were actually giving me permission. They would say things like, "When you're ready to start dating we will support you." As if at 54 years old I needed permission to start dating. The reality is no one has to give you permission to do anything. If you have lost a loved one, what you do regarding your social life is completely up to you. You don't need permission. But for some reason people feel com-pelled to give you permission as if you are asking for it. On the other hand, there will be people who say things to you that imply that they are not giving you permission and that they don't "approve." They will say things like, "Don't you think it's a little bit too soon for you to be thinking about changing jobs?" When people make statements like that I strongly rec-ommend saying very calmly, "No, I don't think it's too soon."

Rule breaker solution: You don't need to offer any explana-tion about what you are doing; you don't have to get permission, because you are an adult.

Rule #6: There are certain things you have to do.

My wife passed away in May, and that following November, my family in Virginia invited me to come for Thanksgiving.

For lots of reasons I did not feel like going to Virginia and I did not feel like celebrating Thanksgiving. I wanted to stay home; I wanted some alone time to think and to work on the house. So I politely declined. When you're grieving it is perfectly OK to choose whether or not to attend holiday functions. It's OK to go to family get-togethers or not go to family get-togethers. At Christmas I did go to Virginia to celebrate with my family.

Rule breaker solution: So aside from taxes and your job responsibilities, just remember that you don't *have to* do anything—particularly when you are grieving. This is, in my opinion, the one time to stop worrying about other people's feelings. It's more important to take care of your own feelings during this difficult time.

Rule #7: You have to start doing something or stop doing something.

Again, we are cast in the role of a griever—people expect us to stop doing things or start doing things. But we don't have to. For example, I have often heard parents who lost children say, "Every year at Halloween my late son and I used to carve a pumpkin and put it on our front porch." My advice when people tell me things like that is, "Well, can you keep doing that until you no longer want to?"

Rule breaker solution: If you have certain traditions, you don't have to stop doing them just because you have a loss. On the other hand, if you have things you want to stop doing— that's perfectly OK as well. The beauty of it all is that it's entirely up to you.

Rule #8: You should or should not cry.

This is by far the most misunderstood element in my opinion about grief. And there are so many odd rules that people have about crying. People, for example, think you should cry a lot in the early days of your grief and maybe not cry at all later into your grief. These are all just such ridiculous concepts it amazes me that we have to even address them, but we do. Crying is extremely therapeutic for releasing the pressure and stress of grief. I have noticed many times after a good, long cry that I felt much better and felt relieved.

The other thing that's interesting about crying is a lot of people don't know how to handle a person who is crying. Particularly when they don't expect it or it seems out of place. I have found in my grief process that I often would start crying when I expected it least. There would be a song that was playing on the radio, a scene in a movie or a TV show, and for some reason something that I heard or saw flipped the trigger that made me cry. I was fortunate that most times I cried, I was not in public.

Rule breaker solution: I want you to give yourself permission to cry in public if it happens—and to not be embarrassed about crying. There is no reason to be embarrassed. It is a normal human function to cry when we are sad or when we are moved in some way. The only reason why crying may sometimes be embarrassing is because of people's awkward reactions to the fact that you're crying. For men who cry (even though I believe this is gradually changing in our society) there is an additional stigma attached to crying. Some men are raised with the philosophy that "boys don't cry" and crying is a sign of weakness and/or emotional vulnerability. Crying is not a sign of weakness and it certainly is a sign of vulnerability, but if you're grieving you're vulnerable—there is nothing wrong with that.

Rule #9: Don't talk about the loss or the person who was lost.

The week after Cindy died I had many people coming to visit the house to pay their respects. Many people would express their condolences and sit quietly talking to the other people who were visiting as well. Not many people asked me what happened as they did not want to appear rude, and of course they didn't want to hurt my feelings by asking me to describe something that was upsetting. However, I am a talker, and I wanted to talk about what happened on Friday night. I also wanted them to know what happened because I knew that they were curious. So I told each person who visited the story, after I asked them if they wanted to know what happened.

Most people seemed appreciative of knowing some of the details about how Cindy passed away. I have two people who are friends of mine who have lost children. The first time I found out that one of my friends had lost a son, I told her that I was sorry and asked her what his name was. She smiled and told me about her son and thanked me for asking about him. She said that most times when she told people that she had lost a son, they got quiet and didn't ask anything for fear of upsetting her. She said, "You know, Shawn, he did exist and I like talking about him." To be clear, there are some people who do not want to talk about their lost loved one and prefer to stay silent about it—that's fine too.

Rule breaker solution: If you want to talk about it—go for it—it may be very helpful.

Rule #10: There is a time frame for grief and it's officially one year.

I have heard people talk about someone who is grieving and say that they have been grieving for ten years and still cry every day. Is that wrong? It's not up to me to say; everyone grieves in a different time frame. On the other hand, I've had people who have insinuated that I was not spending enough time on my grief and suggested that I was maybe moving forward a little too quickly. Now they did not say it in those words, but they insinuated or hinted around about it. I got the message loud and clear. There is no time frame for grief, and there is no time frame for getting over it because you don't get over it. You learn to accept it, but only because you don't have a choice. I will say that if someone is struggling after a great deal of time and is having difficulty managing their life because they are crying and massively depressed, then they may want to seek help in the form of a grief counseling group or individual counseling with a mental health professional.

Grief is not like a highway on a roadmap. I can't look at the map and tell someone, "OK, this map is 100 miles and based on your average speed you'll complete the journey within 12 months." There is no road, there is no map, and there has been a wreck, so no one can say how long the journey is going to take. The other question is, what do we mean by a time frame for grief? That would mean that at some point the grief is totally and completely over, for us never to have another sad feeling again about the loss of a loved one. That, of course, is an absurd concept and will never happen. I find that even though I have healed very nicely in 22 months, there are still days where I see something or hear something or read something and it makes me sad, because it reminds me yet again of my tragic loss.

Rule breaker solution: Take your time—it's all up to you.

Rule #11: Only negative things come out of grief and loss.

Is it possible, even staring into the face of death, that something positive can come out of it? Yes, as terrible as it sounds, I think that good things can come out of bad. Everything in life has a dark side and a light side, a yin and a yang, a black and a white. So the negative obviously is the fact that I lost my wife of 32 years. I'm sure many people say that there couldn't possibly be any positives that came out of that experience, but I would have to disagree. I learned a great deal about appreciating life. I learned a great deal about making sure that every minute I'm on the planet counts. I learned a great deal about not wasting time. I learned a great deal about how I treat others. I have grown even closer to my daughter. I could go on for pages and pages about some of the valuable life lessons that I learned from the death of my wife. So this is the point—are there any positives that may have come out of your experience? It may be something that you've learned, something that you have changed, or a different way that you've approached life that was positive. Just know that most people will not understand your describing a positive in the negative of the death of a loved one. So openly share this information with close friends who understand you, know you, and love you because others will misinterpret what you're saying.

Rule breaker solution: Find the light and the positive.

Rule #12: Happiness and grief can't exist at the same time.

The reality is that happiness and grief can exist at the same time and they do. They are not mutually exclusive. Why is that? I can only tell you what I've learned from my experience. Obviously, I grieved mightily for the death of my wife. What I found was that although I was grieving, there were places and times when I could be happy. It might be watching a movie for a few hours; it might be having dinner with a close friend for a few hours. It might be being engrossed in an excellent book and forgetting about my troubles.

Rule breaker solution: Even though you are grieving a tremendous loss, I would encourage you to find places of happiness within the scope of the grief. People could legitimately say, "How can you be happy at a time like this?" My response to that statement would be, "When am I supposed to be happy? How much later?" It's as if the people say because I choose to have some moments of happiness that means that I loved my wife less or that I'm grieving her less or that I valued her less. It's just that if life is a choice, I'm going to choose to find happiness where and when I can. I choose the light over the darkness.

So those are the silly rules, at least as defined by our society at large. Oh, they just don't know what they do—do they?

Remember, they are your rules *to break;* so live your new life to the fullest.

> "The world is indeed full of peril and in it there are many dark places. But still there is much that is fair. And though in all lands, love is now mingled with grief, it still grows, perhaps, the greater."
>
> —J.R.R. Tolkien, *The Lord of the Rings*

Chapter 8

TAKING CARE OF YOU

"A desire to be in charge of our own lives, a need for control, is born in each of us. It is essential to our mental health, and our success, that we take control." —Robert Foster Bennett

ONCE ALL THE NOISE DIES DOWN, EVERYONE YOU KNOW will go back to their daily lives. It's not that they will forget about you (they love you), but they have families and their work, so they will go back to their regularly scheduled life. It is the nature of the human condition. Here is the catch: they will have a life to go back to; you won't because your loss has changed your life forever. You are building a new life, but it is still under construction. So my point is, in the early days people will take very good care of you, and you will be amazed at the help people will provide. You may be overwhelmed at their generosity of spirit (I was). At some point—they will not be able to take care of you any longer, and they will go back to their daily lives.

Then guess what? It will be up to you to take care of yourself. You will be with you. You will need to stand on your own two feet and deal with life under the most trying of circumstances. But hold fast, you can do it—I know you can do it! I did!

In this chapter I will give you some tools, tips, and techniques for one of the most important parts of the grieving process which is self-care. It is up to you to take good care of yourself so that you can get through this difficult period of loss in your life. It's also important to take care of yourself so you can take care of the people in your life who matter to you. If you are a parent, your kids will need you to take care of them while you are grieving. If you are an older sibling, many will look at you to take a leadership role. You may even get designated as an executor of the estate. The situation doesn't take the responsibility away. Believe me, there were days when I just wanted to scrap it all, sell everything, and move to a small island somewhere.

THE MIND

In my opinion this is the most important tool you have to take care of yourself and your grief. Yes, your old noggin. Many people I talk to as a professional speaker believe that they do not have control over their thinking. The reality is you do have control over your thoughts and your thought processes, and this can really be extremely helpful for you during grief. Don't surrender control and don't think that you don't have control over your thoughts. You are strong and you do have the ability to control what you are thinking. You can't control what has happened (the loss), but you can control how you think about all of it. So here are a few tips for helping to control your thinking as you go through the grief process.

Controlling Your Thoughts

Please don't misunderstand me. I'm not saying that you can't have certain thoughts about the loss of your loved one. I think that is healthy. However, if you constantly sit around thinking about how terrible your loss is, I don't think that is healthy. I know I may face massive criticism by some mental health professionals for saying that, but there you have it—that is my strong opinion. After I lost my wife I had a huge loss and obviously was in a great deal of pain due to her death. I would sit around the house thinking to myself, "How can another human being just disappear so suddenly from the planet? Just be gone?" It was if she had "transported" like they used to do on Star Trek. It was obviously a devastating loss. At a certain point though, I realized that sitting around thinking about my devastating loss was not going to change anything. But what I could change was my thinking. That was a big light bulb for me.

So my suggestion regarding your thinking is that you decide what you want to think about. So instead of focusing on my loss, I would focus on the fact that I had Cindy for 32 years. I can be grateful for the fun times that we had together. I could be grateful for having a long and happy marriage for 32 years. I could be grateful for the daughter who was result of our marriage and still brings me great joy today.

When you have a negative thought, I want you to try to replace it with a positive, counterbalancing thought. Let's say you're grieving the loss of a child. You could say, "I'm so devastated that I lost my child" (which is true), but you can also say how blessed you were to have had the child to begin with and how much sheer joy they brought you when they were alive. I want you to focus on having positive thoughts to counterbalance the negative. I find that it is very helpful in reducing your level of stress.

Avoid Negative Content

When I was in the early days of the grieving process, I made a deliberate attempt to avoid any negative content. Let's face it—if your real life has enough negative content (and boy does it right now), why would you want to expose yourself to more? I avoided all of the news channels (I didn't need to see any stories about death and dying, bombings and blood), all reality shows (the majority of them are intensely negative), any negative books, sad music, and any movies that were negative or had scenes about death and dying. I have always believed in and taught the idea of *garbage in equals garbage out*, and I think it is even truer when you are in a grieving phase of your life. My daughter was very helpful regarding movies—I would call her and ask if she had seen a certain movie or read about it. And often she would say, "Hey Dad, don't go see that movie—in that movie the main character loses his wife." She was my movie-content consultant. So make a conscious effort to avoid all negative content. I think this is a good idea all the time in life (if you want to get and stay motivated), but critically important for your self-care in the early days of grieving.

Consume Positive Content

This is the opposite of the paragraph above. Find content that inspires and motivates or makes you laugh. The idea behind this is to find content that may help strengthen you or make you feel better or make you happy, at least during the time you're being exposed to it. Yes, I know you may say to yourself, "I really don't feel like watching something funny or watching a movie or reading a book that is inspirational." I'm going to ask you to try it—I'm not saying it's a cure, but I am saying that it may help you at least for the short amount of time you're watching, listening, or reading. So find inspirational music, books, and movies that will help you feel better.

Control Your Associations with People

I have often said that "the quality of your life is in direct relation to the quality of the people you associate with." You are in pain and you have had a loss. The last thing you want to do is to associate with people who have negative attitudes, who are mean, or will not support or strengthen you. I want you to carefully evaluate everyone who is in your life personally and professionally. Decide whether each person in your life is a positive influence or a negative influence. I strongly recommend that you not associate with any of the negative people. Get rid of them. You are already grieving and they will drag you down with them into the abyss on the dark side because that's what they do. You don't need them!

Please be exceedingly careful with whom you associate during this time. This is a form of protection. You want to be with people who make you feel better, not worse; who lift you up, not drag you down; and will encourage you, not discourage you. There are people who often object to this concept because they feel they have to associate with negative people who are friends or family. Wrong! You don't have to do anything! Right now you're going through a very tough time in your life; you are grieving a loss. You have the right to take care of yourself by eliminating negative people in your life. You are the architect of your own life, and you decide who you want to be in your life and out of your life. Don't let other people decide for you (who your friends will be and which family members you spend time with). That decision is entirely up to you. This is the one time in your life when it is perfectly OK to be completely, totally selfish and do things for your own reasons and not for someone else's. I promise it will help you heal.

Continue Learning and Studying

I have always been an avid reader of books—particularly books relating to self-improvement and motivation. I also enjoy fiction, books about history, invention, and creativity. I could spend a small fortune just in a few hours at a book store. I also love learning online and love watching documentaries about a whole range of topics. I would encourage you during this time to continue learning and studying about any topic that you're interested in. With the library, the Internet, bookstores, book readers, and Amazon.com, there is no limit to how much information is available to you quickly and often at no or little cost. So put together a plan of study and determine what it is you want to learn and what it is you want to study.

You may want to try attending a noncredit class on a topic you have a passion for at a local university. I found learning and studying to be tremendously stimulating and helpful to me in healing during my most difficult period of grieving. I often try to figure out why it was so helpful. If I had to venture a guess, I would say because it felt like I was moving forward and I was learning something new. Obviously, it also helped take my mind off of my day-to-day grief and allowed me to focus on something else.

Make Up Your Mind

Did you ever notice how when you make up a bed in the morning it just looks so much more appealing when you go to bed at the end of the day? I think you could also do the same thing with your mind. You can decide in your mind that you're going to grow, move forward, and not wallow in your grief. Now I will admit that many people say to me, "How is it that you can just decide on how you're going to think?" I believe it's all just a question of attitude. You can literally make up your mind to do anything you want.

You can either make up your mind to be down, depressed, and sad, or you can make up your mind to be working toward being happy. You'll notice I didn't say that you will be happy right away; I said you're working toward being happy. It is a future goal. During my most intense period of grieving, I always thought and knew that eventually I would one day again be happy. You see, grief is something that happens to us as a result of loss. We obviously can't control that the loss happens, but we can control how we respond to the loss every day. So I want you to make up your mind to work at being happy, not at being sad. You really can decide what you want your attitude to be.

Comparison

Please be careful about comparing yourself to others while you are grieving. In my early days of grief I used to watch couples at the airport and I would say to myself, "Why does he get to have a wife when my wife died? That is so unfair." It was true—it was unfair. If we look carefully at the facts no one on the earth can tell me why his wife is alive and mine died. No one has that answer. It is a great mystery of life. So if it is a great mystery that has no answer—why compare? Why beat your head against the wall? Why ask, "Why does one family lose two children and another family has five healthy kids?" I don't know and neither do you. So my point is that comparison is a very destructive and jealous, negative thought process. It will just tear you apart. So I simply stopped comparing myself to others. It has no value to you and just makes you feel worse, not better.

THE BODY

Your Body and Fitness

When I lost my wife I was overweight, and I lost eight pounds in the first week because I did not feel like eating at all. The week after that I decided to start working out on a regular and consistent basis. As I mentioned in an earlier chapter, I found the workouts to be a big help. It helped boost my morale and my energy level. It also made me feel better about myself. I urge you as part of your healing process to consider some form of regular exercise. It is also one of the best ways to take care of yourself. Will you always feel like working out? Nope. But get yourself up off the couch and work out anyway. I found even when I didn't feel like doing it, I was always glad afterward that I did.

Diet and Nutrition

You have been going through a great deal of stress emotionally, and that means your body has been going through a great deal of stress as well. Try to eat the healthiest selections you can find. When you are eating well, you're taking good care of your body physically, and fruits, vegetables, and vitamins will help you feel better. Oh sure, a glazed doughnut may be comfort food but will not make you feel better in the long run. I also strongly advise against drinking while you are grieving. All drinking does when you're grieving is cover up the problem that you're having—it's the worst form of escapism. Also, alcohol is a depressant which makes you feel more down, not up. Using alcohol to ease your suffering is like putting a Band-Aid on it and not addressing the real issue.

Recreation and Hobbies

A lot of people tell me that when they're participating in their favorite sports or hobbies, time tends to disappear. I want you to think about reengaging with some hobbies or recreational activities that maybe you haven't done for a while. Maybe you love bowling and would love to join a bowling league, or take up golf again or sailing, Frisbee golf, or karate. It doesn't matter what the activity is, as long as it is a hobby or a recreation that you enjoy and love doing.

After my wife passed away I re-embraced playing the drums. I already had a beautiful set of electronic drums—I just had not played them for a while. Going into my drum room and playing the drums for about 30 minutes I found was extremely therapeutic. The sound is also amazing and joyful! I guess it makes sense that hitting big rubber disks hard with sticks would be a great stress reducer. Deciding to participate again in a recreational activity or hobby actually has four benefits:

1. It reduces your level of stress.

2. It takes your mind off of your current situation of loss.

3. In many cases the hobby or recreation may involve socializing with other people which can be great.

4. You get to reconnect with the joy of that hobby.

So take a look at one or two hobbies or recreational activities that you can reengage in as part of your self-care.

SPIRIT

Social Life

Most people I talk to tell me that their social life changed once they lost a spouse or child. I guess it's because the dynamic of your family has changed, and the people you socialize with don't really know how to deal with your loss. Additionally, if you were originally a couple and you now are single, people you formerly associated with as couples now think of you as single (which you are). In my life, I noticed the social dynamic changed because couples who used to socialize with us no longer did because the "us" was now just a "me." So you'll come to a juncture where you'll need to reevaluate your social life and decide who you will be socializing with (and who you won't).

Some people will stop socializing with you because they feel uncomfortable, and some people will stop associating with you because it is just a normal turn of events. They don't mean anything by it, it just happens. I learned that when you change and your life changes, everybody else around you changes as well, even if they don't know it—they do. If the people who used to socialize with you no longer do, I urge you to still make an effort to socialize. You may want to join a civic group (such as the Moose, Eagles, or Jaycees). You may want to get involved with a religious group of your choosing at your church, or you may want to get involved with social groups like those you can find on Meetup.com.

I do strongly encourage you to re-embrace your social life because you really do need to be around people, particularly when you are grieving. In the early days of my grieving I joined a Meet Up group that was for widows and widowers. This group held numerous social events every week for people who were widows and/or widowers. They emphasized the fact that it was not a dating group, but a social group for single people to get together without the pressure of a dating-type situation. I did go on a hike with my Meet Up group and had a really good time just talking to other people and socializing. This group had trips to the movies, to museums, and often met at restaurants for group dinners or other planned social functions every week. So take the time to find groups you can socialize with, because it will help you heal during your grieving.

Spiritual

When I lost my wife, I felt a need to reconnect with my spirituality. I found some local churches in the area and started visiting them. I can't really explain why I felt a strong need to make the spiritual connection—I just did and I didn't question it. At one church I visited I had an unusual experience when I ran into a woman who used to be our next-door neighbor. She approached me and said hello and asked me how Cindy was doing. Sadly, I had to tell her that Cindy passed away, which was a little bit awkward for me and for her as well, because it only happened a few months before. Did that uncomfortable experience stop me from visiting that church again? No. Did that experience stop me from visiting other churches? Absolutely not! I kept at it because I felt like belonging to a church would be helpful for me.

This is not a religious book in any way shape or form, so how you define spirituality is entirely up to you. You may define spirituality as attending a church or synagogue or mosque. On the other hand, you may define spirituality as meditating or practicing yoga, or just reading spiritual materials. The rest is up to you (the how), but really think about engaging with the spiritual side of life during your grieving process. In my opinion it helps you in three ways.

1. You may find it comforting in many ways.

2. You will have the opportunity to be around other people.

3. You may find social activities that will help you as well.

Relaxation Techniques

I also urge you at this time to think about things you do to relax. It may be taking a warm bath, going for a hike on a nature trail, sitting by the ocean, swimming in a pool, or lighting candles. Try to do some relaxing activities a couple times a week in order to help burn off some of your stress that is a result of grief. It is up to you to manage your stress. (It's called stress management.) For me it was working out or reading a really good book, as well as doing activities from my joy list, which I mentioned in a previous chapter.

It is important to schedule relaxation into your week so that you can practice good stress management. I found when I went to our local pool for a few hours and lay in the sun, I came back feeling much better having participated in a relaxing activity. Because you will be more stressed as someone who is grieving—also pay careful attention to managing your stress at work. Make sure to take breaks (no one at work takes them anymore!), take lunches away from your desk, and try to get outside when the weather is nice. If someone at work is a big stressor for you, try to spend less time around them if you can.

Sleep

Because grief can be exhausting, you want to pay careful attention to getting enough sleep. When grieving, if you can, you should sleep more not less. That may even mean taking a nap here and there or sleeping in on Saturdays when you never did before. Spoil yourself by investing in some nice pillows, blankets, and linens (you can feel the difference). Use linen spray (it is wonderful for relaxing). Your body needs to recover from the stress. Make your bed a luxurious oasis where you can lie down and truly relax.

So take good care of the one who matters most right now—you.

> Life will break you. Nobody can protect you from that, and living alone won't either, for solitude will also break you with its yearning. You have to love. You have to feel. It is the reason you are here on earth. You are here to risk your heart. You are here to be swallowed up. And when it happens that you are broken, or betrayed, or left, or hurt, or death brushes near, let yourself sit by an apple tree and listen to the apples falling all around you in heaps, wasting their sweetness. Tell yourself you tasted as many as you could.
>
> —LOUISE ERDRICH, *The Painted Drum*

CHAPTER 9

WHERE YOU ARE: THE COMPASS

"This is how you survive the unsurvivable, this is how you lose that which you cannot bear to lose, this is how you reinvent yourself, overcome your abusers, fulfill your ambitions and meet the love of your life: by following what is true, no matter where it leads you." —AUGUSTEN BURROUGHS

YOU WERE AT A CERTAIN POINT IN YOUR LIFE, AND SUDdenly everything changed. Overnight, it seems, you lost a loved one. It's as if your life was a voyage and you were headed in a certain direction, and suddenly everything changed and the voyage is completely different. The map was destroyed. It's as if the compass got completely smashed and tossed aside, thrown out, and you have no direction.

In this chapter, I would like to talk about where you are and where you're going and where you want to be.

Do you remember when you were a kid and people asked you what you wanted to be when you grew up? You would smile and say you wanted to be a fireman or a doctor or a schoolteacher. You knew what you wanted.

This is kind of the same question—except it's rephrased as, "What do you want to do now?" You have had a catastrophic loss—the question is, what will your life look like now? In Chapter 5 I talked about needing to make some difficult decisions on a daily basis. I know that you have been making some of those decisions already; this chapter is about getting more into a "planning mindset," to think about what you are going to do going forward short term, midterm, and long term.

I know this is so hard, and you wish you could change it back and make it all go away and make everything like it once was; but that is not your or my reality. The reality is everything has changed and everything in your life has changed as a result of your loss. I sincerely and honestly believe that if you can get into a mindset where you are thinking about the future it will help you heal. It will also help you make better decisions if you know where it is that you're headed and what those decisions are based on. As my sister-in-law said to me in the early days of grief, "Well, what choice do we have? We just need to keep moving forward." This is your version of moving forward and getting into the planning mindset, the proactive mindset, the positive mindset. This is also a unique opportunity to determine how you want to reinvent yourself and how you want to reinvent your life based on the situation you are in now.

So I want you to set aside some quiet thinking time when you can pause and reflect and really evaluate where you are in every part of your life. Socrates once said, "The unexamined life is not worth living." So it is now up to you to do the hard work, the thinking work, the planning work to determine your road moving forward. You can do it, I know you can—because I did.

I would urge you to sit down and do this work sooner rather than later. Oh, I know you don't feel like doing it—you are grieving. I get it. But putting your head in the sand and ignoring it is not going to make any of these situations go away, and in fact they will get worse. So don't procrastinate, and be proactive in looking at each area of your life now to determine what it is you want to do.

I want you to take a look at every part of your life currently, in every category. Pull out a pen and paper, an iPad, or a rock and a chisel—it doesn't matter to me which one you pick just as long as you start to write these things down.

Let's take an in-depth look at each one.

FINANCIAL

This is the time in your life to really take a look at where you are financially. After my wife passed away I was very fortunate that I was in good shape financially in terms of having money in the bank, having a successful business, and not having to worry about where the next dollar was coming from. I was very fortunate in that regard. Because I was financially sound, I did not have to make any major financial decisions at that time because everything was being paid and there were no bill collectors nipping at my heels. So here are some areas of finance to look at:

- What is my level of debt?

- How much cash do I have on hand in savings or checking?

- Do I have bills which are going to be due short term or long term which may be problematic?

- Has the loss of my loved one affected my overall income? For example, if I had passed away instead of my wife, she would have been severely affected financially because Cindy did not work outside of the home. I was the sole breadwinner of the house. So even though I had a fairly large life insurance policy, she would have had to reevaluate what she was going to do to make a living—because she could not have lived off the life insurance forever. So for her, the effect on her overall income would've been dramatic; for me it was not dramatic at all.

- What are your current expenses for mortgage/rent and other household expenses? Are you able to pay these bills without struggling? For example, you may find that you're not able to pay your current mortgage or rent by yourself. This may put you into a situation where you have to sell your current home, move out of your apartment, or advertise for a roommate who can share expenses.

- Are there future expenses that you will need to prepare for? For example, you may have a child who is getting close to college age and you may need to pay for school, or you may have a home that has a roof that will eventually need to be replaced in the next five years.

- Would you like to indulge in something? Maybe you have always dreamed of going to Paris, or signing up for gourmet cooking classes, or going on some sort of wild safari adventure. If you have the wherewithal financially, are you interested in indulging in something that you've always wanted to do?

- What are your financial goals short term, midterm, and long term? How have they changed as a result of your loss?

- Are there any other things financially that you need to start thinking about now?

PHYSICAL HEALTH

As I have outlined in earlier chapters, I decided that one of my large goals after my wife passed away was to become less large. So I joined Weight Watchers, consistently worked out every week, and ended up losing a total of 54 pounds. I can tell you that losing the weight was a tremendous boost to my self-esteem. Once I lost the weight I was constantly getting compliments about how I looked, and was able to invest in an entirely new wardrobe, which I must admit was a lot of fun.

My daughter was initially concerned that my response to grief would be the opposite—that I would become less active because I was grieving, and work out less, eat more, and gain even more weight. So she was definitely concerned about my health. If you are grieving, I think it is essential to look after your physical fitness and health. There is an old saying I have heard many times which is "you are as good as you feel." I would change that saying around and say "you can make yourself feel good." The battering emotion of grief can be emotionally and physically draining. Help yourself and those you support and love by battling grief by getting in shape or maintaining your healthy body.

Here are some questions to ask yourself to analyze where you are currently in relation to your physical health.

- Where are you at physically? Are you the perfect weight, underweight, or overweight?
- How do you feel about your current shape?
- Do you work out on a regular and consistent basis?
- Do you do anaerobic exercise?
- Do you do aerobic exercise?
- Do you have the resources to work out regularly (gym, home gym, other fitness equipment, hiking trails, etc.)?
- What are your fitness goals?
- Can you make the time to work out two to three times a week? Are there any new fitness routines or programs you would like to try, but you haven't (like Zumba or Cross Fit)?
- If you want to lose weight, how much weight do you want to lose?

- Do you have a diet or nutrition plan that you followed in the past successfully?
- What are your specific health and fitness goals short term?
- What are your specific health and fitness goals long term?
- How has your loss affected this area?
- Why is this important to you right now?

SOCIAL

When you go from being married to being single as a widow or widower, your social life will change dramatically with your new label. If you become a parent who has lost a child, your social life will also change dramatically. If you're someone who has lost a dear friend, that can also change your social life and social circle. So now is the time to really evaluate where you are socially.

It is tempting to just stay home. It is tempting to just sit on the couch and watch endless TV shows and not go anywhere. It is hard to go to a social event as a widow or widower, particularly for the first couple of times that you go. But you're going to have to put on your suit of armor, get ready for the event, and walk into a social event even though you don't feel like doing it at all. Why? Because you need to push yourself in order to become social, so that you can eventually feel comfortable being social again.

I was very fortunate that in my early days of grief I had several friends reach out to me to encourage me to be social.

My friend Darlene and her husband asked me to have dinner with them one evening. When I asked her why they wanted to have dinner, she said very simply, "Well, you need to get out of the house, silly!" I must confess that afternoon as I was getting dressed to go to dinner I didn't feel like going. I put one foot in front of the other and forced myself to go. I felt like a third wheel, a single man having dinner with a married couple. I can tell you this—we had a very nice time, and afterward I was very glad that I went, so getting outside of my early comfort zone paid off. For the first several months of your new social life it will be weird and a bit awkward, but that is to be expected. The good news is you will find your footing and you will eventually feel more comfortable. I promise.

There are two elements to your social life:

1. Your general social life (socializing with friends and family).

2. Your romantic social life (dating and love relationships).

Your General Social Life

Take some time to think about where you can socialize with others. You may want to get involved in social events at your former university (like alumni associations), you may want to get involved with fraternal organizations (Lions, Elks, Jaycees), or with religious organizations or clubs at your respective churches. You may want to get involved in local politics or historical associations. Heck, you can even join a hockey league—that's a great way to meet people.

When my parents relocated to Virginia, they decided to join the Moose Lodge and the church. Joining the Moose Lodge allowed them to meet many of their friends and neighbors who lived in the area, and they also made many new friends at their church.

Here are some questions to ask yourself:

- What are some organizations where I can meet and socialize with others?
- What are activities that I enjoy doing that also could have a social component? (A volleyball league, for example.)
- What kind of people do I want to meet? Why?
- Who should I reconnect with now?
- What is the age range of people I want to meet and socialize with?
- Are there any hobbies that I enjoy but also could have a social component? (Such as a book club.)
- Are there any online groups that I could join to help me socialize both online and in person? (Like meetup.com, for example.)
- Why is it important for me to socialize?
- What are my goals in socializing?
- How has my loss affected this area?
- Why is this important to me right now?

Your Romantic Social Life

As outlined in a prior chapter, I made very specific decisions about when I was ready to start dating. So I really want you to look into your heart and determine how soon and when you would like to think about reengaging in a romantic relationship. I do not believe that people are meant to live alone—ever.

I do believe that many widows and widowers have a very strong belief that if they begin dating, it is a sign of disrespect to the one they lost. Please reconsider this thought process because it is so wrong and so damaging to you on a personal level. It is not disloyal to seek the companionship of another person after your loved one has passed away.

Everyone I have talked to believes that the loved one who has departed would want you to be happy. I believe that the loved one who has departed would not want you to be lonely and sad. In my conversations with widows and widowers they often say to me, "I just can't imagine being with someone else," or, "I can't imagine holding someone else's hand or going out on a date with someone else—it just seems weird and awkward and wrong." I will say to you that it certainly does at first feel weird. It does in the beginning feel awkward. But it is not wrong. You are single—morally, socially, and legally single. When you date for a little while, the nature of your humanity takes over and it feels OK to be holding someone else's hand—and then it feels more than OK—it feels great!

I'm going to be blunt—it absolutely sucks to come home to an empty household. It hurts to lie in an empty bed at night. It is an empty feeling to go on a business trip and know that you have no one to call to tell them that you arrived safely. It is a terrible feeling to know that you no longer have a loved one to be concerned about you. So my question to you is, why would you want to continue to maintain a lonely lifestyle when there are people out there in the world who could bring you great joy and happiness?

Look—life is short, we both know that. And if life is short, should we not try to seek out as much happiness and joy as possible? I can't tell you what is right for you. I just want you to consider the possibility that you can love again. If you do fall in love again, it does not mean that you did not love the person you were in love with originally. I believe that you could have enough room in your life to love two people, or maybe even three people. Is love in such short supply, or is love unlimited? I believe that love is unlimited, and I could have loved one woman and also end up loving another woman later in my life. The love of each one does not nullify the love of the other.

Here are some questions to ask yourself:

- Are you willing to take a risk on love again?
- What are the risks?
- When do you feel like you would be ready to date again if you are a widow or widower?
- Who would be the kind of person you would be looking for?
- How do you feel about the idea of being with another person?
- Would you like to be in love again?
- Do you feel as if loving another person would be disrespectful to the one you lost?

- How would you go about finding someone to date?
- Would you be open to joining singles groups?
- Would you be open to joining online dating sites (like eHarmony)?
- Have you spoken to any of your friends or family about this issue?
- Do you feel like there's someone you need permission from to start dating?
- How would people in your family feel about you dating?
- What do you think would be the timing?
- What would you get from dating?
- How has your loss affected this area?
- Why is this important to you right now?

Please don't overlook this very important aspect of your social life. You have been through enough pain. If there's anyone on the planet who deserves to be happy—you, of all people, deserve to be happy. The choice is up to you. Think about it.

FAMILY

There is no question in my mind that when you have a loss, the entire dynamic of your family will change. My wife Cindy has a brother and a sister, and of course they were my brother- and sister-in-law. But here is my question—what are they now? Are they still my brother- and sister-in-law? Are they my "ex-brother- and sister-in-law"? Are they my "former brother- and sister-in-law"? I have not seen them in over 22 months, since my wife passed away. Admittedly, both of them live in other states. I have found that with the distance of time, the number of e-mails and phone calls have dramatically reduced.

I think this is just a natural function of what happens. The dynamics of the relationship changed because Cindy passed away. She was really the connection between me and my in-laws. That connection is lost. We have just naturally drifted apart, and that is OK. I bring this up because I want you to be aware of how the family dynamic will change as a result of loss—because it will change. Don't be surprised by it—it just happens. It is neither a good thing nor a bad thing. It's just the way it works; it's human nature. That being said, I do think you need to decide who you will continue to associate with in your immediate and extended family. Here are some questions to consider:

- Who do I want to maintain contact with?
- Who do I not want to maintain contact with?
- How will I communicate this information?
- How do I think the dynamics will change?
- Which family members do I think will stop associating with me? Why?
- How will this family dynamic affect others around me (children, siblings, etc.)?
- How has my loss affected this area?
- Why is this important to me right now?

WORK

Sometimes when people have a loss, they continue to do the job they have always done. I am a professional speaker and a book author, and it's how I continue to make my living today. After my wife passed away, I never considered changing my profession, because I love what I do. However, sometimes after people have had a significant loss in their life they decide that they want to do a different kind of work, new work, or change careers. The decision should be purely up to you. So here are some questions to ask yourself:

- Do I love the work that I do currently?
- Do I want to continue in this line of work?
- Do I want to change my work?
- When do I want to retire?
- If I was going to change my work, would I change where I work or the kind of work I do?
- Do I want to change careers?
- Am I currently happy with the work I am doing? Why?
- Am I currently unhappy with the work I'm doing?
- What kind of work would I be doing if there were no restrictions or limitations?
- What is my dream job?
- What work do I want to do short term, midterm, and long term?
- How has my loss affected this area?

- Why is this important to me right now?

SPIRITUAL LIFE

I have spoken with many people who, in experiencing grief, decided to embrace spirituality in more depth. I've also spoken with people experiencing grief who have not embraced spirituality and actually went in the other direction and became less spiritual. I have talked to people who turned more to God and some who became really angry at God. I can't judge anyone. No matter your religious/spiritual perspective, it is another area of your life to look at. Here are some questions to contemplate:

- How do I feel about my spiritual life right now?
- Do I want to get more involved? Why?
- Do I want to get less involved? Why?
- Why is this important to me right now?
- How could it help me?

So these are the most important areas to look at now. These are all central to analyzing where you are and where you want to be. These will help you navigate the waters of your new life.

Finally, I want you to live the life you want to live—and to take control. Grief doesn't have to own your whole life. Look grief in the face and say, "You don't own my life, you know—you are just renting!"

Here is a great poem from Ellen Bass:

THE THING IS

to love life, to love it even
when you have no stomach for it
and everything you've held dear
crumbles like burnt paper in your hands,
your throat filled with the silt of it.
When grief sits with you, its tropical heat
thickening the air, heavy as water
more fit for gills than lungs;
when grief weights you like your own flesh
only more of it, an obesity of grief,
you think, How can a body withstand this?
Then you hold life like a face
between your palms, a plain face,
no charming smile, no violet eyes,
and you say, yes, I will take you
I will love you, again.

—ELLEN BASS

CHAPTER 10

A STORY OF HOPE AND LOVE

"For what it's worth: it's never too late or, in my case, too early to be whoever you want to be. There's no time limit, stop whenever you want. You can change or stay the same, there are no rules to this thing. We can make the best or the worst of it. I hope you make the best of it. And I hope you see things that startle you. I hope you feel things you never felt before. I hope you meet people with a different point of view. I hope you live a life you're proud of. If you find that you're not, I hope you have the courage to start all over again."
—ERIC ROTH, *The Curious Case of Benjamin Button* screenplay

I WROTE THIS BOOK TO HELP PEOPLE WHO ARE GRIEVING, but I also wrote this book to help people grieving to know that there is hope for a brighter future! There really is a light at the end of this tunnel you are in. Yes, you can have a new life and if you so choose—you can possibly find love again.

As I mentioned in an earlier chapter I had in-depth discussions with my best friend Dave about dating, and in late August of 2013 I decided to be brave and dive into the dating pool.

I decided the best approach for me was online dating. Besides, where does someone my age meet women who are my age and available? At first I found the world of online dating to be confusing; after all, there were so many choices with websites like match.com, ourtime.com, seniorpeoplemeet.com, and eHarmony.com. Which one was the best for me? I really didn't know. After doing research for a couple of weeks, I determined that the two that were probably best suited for me were eHarmony and seniorpeoplemeet.com; because as much as I hated to admit it, I was 54 years old, so I qualified in the category of senior (I don't like that label).

So I went on both sites, filled out my profiles, posted my pictures, and nervously pushed the right buttons (I hoped). The thing I was most surprised by was the rapid speed in which the systems worked. Within a few days I started getting notifications saying that I had matches on seniorpeoplemeet.com and I had matches on eHarmony. It was an odd feeling every morning to get up and realize that there were five or six women on each site—either ones I had been matched to on eHarmony or who were especially interested in me on Senior People Meet. So I started reviewing each of my matches because I was extremely curious to see who and what type of person I would be attracted to and what those ladies were like.

Some of my experiences bordered on hilarious. One woman who said that she was interested in me sent an e-mail and I e-mailed her back, and we started an e-mail discussion on

Senior People Meet. She seemed like a nice woman in my age range and was attractive. She seemed to be fairly successful. We then set up a phone call for the following weekend. On our phone call, she complained nonstop for the first 45 minutes about how terrible her weekend had been and said she had the "worst weekend ever." She then described herself as an optimist and a successful person who had been married several times.

After 50 minutes, she finally asked me to tell her a little bit about myself. To me she seemed totally self-absorbed and a very negative person. At the end of the phone call she said, "Well Shawn, what do you think?" I asked her what she meant. She said, "What do you think about us going out?" I asked her what she thought, and she said, "I would love to go out with you!" I then told her that I never made any snap decisions and needed to give it some thought overnight. I was new to this online dating thing, and I did not want to hurt her feelings.

The next night I called her back and told her I'd given it serious consideration, and to me it felt like for lots of reasons we were just not a fit. When she asked me why, I told her that I thought she just had too much drama going on in her life (not her fault), and I was looking for someone whose life was a little calmer at that point. She got a little irritated with me, then said she appreciated that. It took guts to call her back to turn her down. She also told me she saw several "red flags" about me too. When I asked what they were, she said I was a "new widower." I told her I understood that being a legitimate concern. So that was my weird and disappointing start to my online dating experience.

Over several weeks I continued to correspond with nice ladies on both sites. I finally found someone who seemed to be very nice, and we had several in-depth e-mails back and forth and ended up talking on the phone. I had my first date with Justine (not her real name) about one week later. We had a great date, we got along well, and we laughed a lot and had a good time. My first date was a real eye opener for me because I found that I felt completely comfortable being around another woman. I didn't feel awkward and everything felt pretty natural and normal.

We proceeded to date for about two months, but it just didn't work out for lots of reasons. Our political beliefs were very different. She had children at home and I had a grown child. I was calm and she was very high-strung. I also realized that with her being a single mom, she had responsibilities for work, for teenage children, bills, running a household, etc. She also told me that her daughter was on a traveling sports league and there would be several weekends that she would not be able to see me.

So I pretty quickly got the message that I was not going to be number one in her life. I was going to be number eight or nine behind all of her many priorities, which I understood. It just wasn't the kind of relationship that I was looking for. I needed to be number one in someone's life. She wanted to date, I wanted a relationship. I bore her no ill-will or bad feelings—it just didn't work out and wasn't meant to be.

Prior to dating Justine, I had been matched with a beautiful woman on eHarmony named Rachael, and I sent her an e-mail saying hello. Unfortunately, I did not get a response—and based on her picture and profile, I was a little disappointed. As luck would have it, about two months later I got a response from Rachael saying that she would love to exchange information on eHarmony. She had been really busy and had not had time to be on the website for a few months.

This woman, Rachael, had really gotten my attention in every way, so I thought I would check out where she lived in terms of geographic location. I noticed her profile said East Greenville, Pennsylvania. Disturbingly, when I googled Greenville, Pennsylvania, I saw that it was five hours from where I live. I then sent Rachael a very kind e-mail saying that unfortunately, eHarmony had made a big mistake and that where she lived was five hours away from my home and I really was not interested in dating somebody who lives so far away. Rachael kindly e-mailed me back and told me that indeed *Greenville,* Pennsylvania was five hours away, but her location of *East Greenville,* Pennsylvania was only about an hour from my house. Besides, that was her work location, and she actually lived in the same county as me, Chester County, Pennsylvania. Wow.

So the confusion about her location actually led to several funny e-mails back and forth, which really broke the ice. Rachael said she was not a huge fan of e-mail and would rather talk on the phone, and we ended up having our first phone conversation on November 23, 2012. She was a real charmer. She was funny, she was articulate, and she was a great conversationalist. Toward the end of the conversation, I looked at my watch and realized that we'd been speaking for two hours. I was so shocked. I said "Oh my gosh, Rachael—I can't believe it—we have been talking on the phone now for almost two hours!"

She blurted out, "I could talk to you forever!" The funny thing was I felt the same way and I said so. From that point forward we ended up talking on the phone every single day until our first date about a week and a half later.

The great thing about our first date was that I felt like our conversations and e-mails had helped me to already know a lot about who she was, and boy, oh boy—this woman really floored me! She was amazing. She met me at a restaurant on Friday night. I got there early and waited for her arrival, nervously pacing in front of the restaurant. She was running a little late because she came straight from work and called me to tell me. I told her to relax and take her time. I watched every car as they pulled up to the restaurant. When I finally saw her pull up and then walk toward the door, I knew immediately from her picture that it was her.

My heart started pounding and my pulse rate went up as I met her at the front door of the restaurant, and she immediately gave me the best hug of my life. I had never been hugged like that—she hugged like she meant it! Our dinner was wonderful. We had an amazing conversation with each other, and we had a lot of fun. In person, she was even more beautiful than her online pictures and had a high level of charisma and energy. She was charming, sweet, and funny.

After having our romantic dinner at the café, we decided to go to Barnes & Noble to look around because we both love reading. So we drove a couple blocks down the street to the bookstore. When we arrived at Barnes & Noble, I suggested that we go upstairs because there were quieter places to talk upstairs. As we were looking for a table where we could sit down, we walked down the motivational book aisle. As we were walking down that aisle, Rachael stopped and said, "Oh look, here is one of your books." One of my motivational books was sitting on the shelf with the cover facing outward—a rather unusual sighting because most books are stacked so that the spines are facing outward, making it harder for a book to stand out. But these books were stacked covers out, so they were much more noticeable as you went by. Rachael was obviously impressed to see one of my books in stock at Barnes and Noble. It was funny because it seemed like such a setup, that maybe that's where I took all of my dates so that they could see my books! (Not true!)

We sat in the bookstore talking and talking until Barnes & Noble closed, although it seemed like we were in the bookstore for only a few minutes. We then drove back to the restaurant and sat in my car talking until two o'clock in the morning. Each hour Rachael would say, "Well, I should probably go—it's eleven o'clock—probably past your bedtime."

I would say, "Would you like to talk a little longer?"

She would say, "Yes." Finally, at two o'clock in the morning I thought I should let her go—but only because I thought she would think I was a crazy man if I suggested we talk any longer. I drove home that night thinking and knowing that something amazing had happened. I was falling in love with Rachael. I just knew she was "the one."

On Memorial Day weekend of 2013, Rachael and I went and visited my parents and the rest of my family in Virginia. She met them for the first time. They had the same reaction to her as I did—they fell madly in love with her too. We left my mom and dad's house in Smith Mountain Lake, Virginia, and I told Rachael I wanted her to see the famous Mill Mountain Star in Roanoke on the way out. It is the world's largest man-made illuminated star. It sits on top of the mountain overlooking Roanoke, Virginia and lights up at night. It has been there a long time and is an icon of the star city.

We stopped at the star on top of Mill Mountain. The weather was beautiful, sunny, and about 78 degrees. It was a gorgeous day, the kind of day the chamber of commerce would order if they could. We took in the view and walked a few of the trails. When we came back to the area with the famous star, I told her I wanted to take another picture with the star behind her. As she stood where she would be posing, she turned to get the camera to hand it to me. When she turned around, I was on one knee with a ring box in my hand and said, "Rachael, I have a question for you—will you marry me?" For some reason she said yes! Three times!

As I was asking the big question, I didn't realize that about 15 feet away several people were sitting on a bench quietly watching the whole scene play out. We became the afternoon's star attraction. A lovely senior couple from Louisville, Kentucky came over and said they wanted to introduce themselves and be "the first to congratulate us." They had been married for over 45 years and hoped we would be as happy as they were.

It made that special moment even more special and poignant; they were such a very sweet couple. We had someone take a picture of us with them and Rachael sent them a nice note with a print of the picture. Many others came over to congratulate us and they were all so very excited for us. So the day of our engagement we will never forget, and whenever we drive up to the Roanoke, Virginia area we will always see "our" star, which marks a very important day in our lives. I told Rachael I wanted to ask her somewhere very special, a one-of-a-kind place, and besides she was my star.

We will be getting married on February 28, 2014. I am so honored to have her as my wife. I feel so very blessed.

So why do I share this story with you? To let you know that you can live again, breathe again, play again, have joy again, have love again, laugh again, and be happy again after any loss. I am proof of that. In order to do that, you have to have courage—the courage to take risks, the courage to be willing to feel again, the courage to honor the past but embrace the future, the courage to move forward without knowing what will happen. Take a risk and roll the dice. You have to have initiative and be willing to take action. You have to be proactive. Join a gym, join a dating site online, join a singles group, join a league, get a matchmaker, join a social club, join the golf club, join a support group, but just do something. Life is too short to sit around and be miserable, sad, and alone. At the end of your life, I don't want you to regret the steps you could have taken. Do it now, not later.

I have met many people who have said after hearing my story that they "could never do online dating," or "I am just too shy," or "why would I want to meet a stranger online?" Well, everyone you have ever known was a stranger before you knew them!

The story I just related is about finding a new love interest, but don't miss the point of the story—it is about hope and new beginnings. That could apply whether you lost a child, a friend, or a family member.

Every day the sun still rises. You can either turn and face it, or hide in the dark. The sun is better for you, trust me.

So how do you get started? It's just like taking a walk— just take the first step. Here are some quick tips to help you get going:

- Make a list: Make a list of some different ways you can get out and meet some people. Take that list and commit to doing one of those things each week.

- Practice positive self-talk: Say to yourself, "I am getting better," and "I am going to feel happier," and "I am going to find someone who I can share my life with."

- Have criteria: Decide who the kind of person is you want to meet and describe them on paper. What they look like, what they believe, what they stand for, what their values are.

- Be flexible: You don't know what life will offer you in terms of opportunity. Be open to the possibilities.

- Be honest: When people ask your story, tell them the truth. If they can't handle your story, then you don't want to be around them anyway.

- Think of it as an adventure: You are going to talk to and meet some really interesting people! You can learn from every one of them. Have fun!

- Do something: You will find, like I did, that when you start doing things you will start to shake off the stagnation.

- Buddy up: If you don't want to go it alone socially, ask a buddy to go with you for moral support when you go to a party or some other social event. Let them be your crutch at first.

- Leave the guilt: Decide to leave the guilt behind—nothing is your fault. There is nothing to feel guilty about at all. Why would you feel guilty when you are not doing anything wrong?

- Try new things: Never bowled before? Go try it. Never gone scuba diving before? Sign up for a class.

- There is no real risk: Going out there and starting to live again has no risks except that you may feel a little awkward at first. You may feel odd, but no one else will know that—only you.

- Do it anyway: You may really not feel like it at first, but do it anyway. You may surprise yourself and enjoy something for a change.

Imagine I am sitting in your living room, and I want you to look at me and hear this message—you can do this. It crushes my heart when I hear of people who have lost a loved one eight or nine years ago, and are still so sad and struggling to get through their days! I don't stand in judgment—my god, what some of us have gone through.

Why does it crush my heart? Because I just feel sad that they have their life in park and are not moving forward, not living—they are just stuck. They have lost the spark of life itself. It doesn't have to be that way. Life is too short to spend a decade grieving. That is such a big chunk of life that has been a blur, a sleepwalking existence.

It is not easy, but you can decide to re-create a new life, a new world, a new spirit within you. Because tomorrow the sun still rises, and it always will.

> Make a radical change in your lifestyle and begin to boldly do things which you may previously never have thought of doing, or been too hesitant to attempt. So many people live within unhappy circumstances and yet will not take the initiative to change their situation because they are conditioned to a life of security, conformity, and conservation, all of which may appear to give one peace of mind, but in reality nothing is more damaging to the adventurous spirit within a man than a secure future. The very basic core of a man's living spirit is his passion for adventure. The joy of life comes from our encounters with new experiences, and

hence there is no greater joy than to have an end-lessly changing horizon, for each day to have a new and different sun. If you want to get more out of life, you must lose your inclination for monotonous security and adopt a helter-skelter style of life that will at first appear to you to be crazy. But once you become accustomed to such a life you will see its full meaning and its incredible beauty.

—JON KRAKAUER, *Into the Wild*

CHAPTER 11

RESOURCES TO HELP YOU

*"We must be willing to let go of the life
we planned so as to have the life that is
waiting for us."* —JOSEPH CAMPBELL

I KNOW THAT LIFE HAS BEEN HARD FOR YOU. YOU ARE HURT-
ing and maybe reeling from everything that has happened
to you, your family, and your life. I feel your pain and hurt.
I really do, because I have been there. Just know this—it does
get better! You will get better! Your life will get better! You
just have to keep moving forward. Imagine a future where you
will be happy again and have joy again. It will happen—but it
won't happen by itself—you have to work at it. Because tomorrow the sun still rises. You can curse the light as being too
bright in your eyes or say, "Good morning sun, thanks for the
warm loving rays you give me!"

I have listed on these next several pages resources for you
to consider, and I hope they help. I can also be a resource
to you. I do private one-on-one coaching and I would be
happy to come and speak at your next company or association

meeting. My e-mail is sldoyle1@aol.com and my phone is 610-857-4742.

In your journey down the road of grief, I am with you and want you to know there are many resources available to you. You can try to go it alone, by why would you? In today's world there are so many resources open and available, both online and in book form. Use the resources out there to give you support for a while. Below are some resources. Some of them are blank for you to fill in—resources you have identified—and some of them are lists based on my research.

Your Network

Who are family and friends who can be your support network? (Write names here.)

_____

_____

_____

_____

Support Groups

There are many support groups both religious and secular. Go online and look for local grief support groups. What are they?

_____

_____

_____

_____

_____

_____

National Grief Support Groups
(WHO OFFER LIVE SUPPORT
OR SOCIAL GROUPS)

Grief Share: (www.griefshare.org)
A faith-based support group for people who are grieving. I did a search on my zip code and found 20 groups nearby.

Compassionate Friends: (www.compassionatefriends.org)
A support group for people who have lost a child. They have lots of chapters all over the United States.

Hospice Foundation of America: (www.hospicefoundation.org)
An organization that offers end-of-life care resources. They also offer many local support groups in many areas.

The National Alliance for Grieving Children:
(www.nationalallianceforgrievingchildren.org)
An organization that supports grieving children. They offer many local support groups as well.

Twinless twins: (www.twinlesstwins.org)
This is a group that supports twins that have lost their twin brother or sister.

AARP: (www.aarp.org/family/lifeafterloss)
Has support for surviving spouses.

The National Widowers' Organization:
(www.nationalwidowers.org)
Supports widowers and has several local support groups around the country.

National resource directory: (www.nrd.gov)
An organization that serves military service members and their families who have lost a loved one. They have many survivor organizations listed on the site.

American Association of Suicidology: (www.suicidology.org)
Offers resources for survivors of suicide and has resources and support groups.

COPS: (www.nationalcops.org)
This group provides resources for families of cops who have been killed in the line of duty. Offers resources and support groups as well as local chapters.

Grief Recovery after a Substance Passing (GRASP):
(www.grasp.org)
A support group for people who have lost a loved one due to substance abuse or addiction. Offers resources and support groups as well as local chapters.

Mothers in Sympathy and Support (MISS):
(www.missfoundation.org)
An organization to support parents after the death of an infant or young child. Offers resources and support groups as well as local chapters.

National Hospice and Palliative Care Organization:
(www.nhpco.org)
A national network of hospice facilities. Offers resources and support groups as well as local chapters.

National Students of Ailing Mothers and Fathers Support Network (AMF): (www.studentsofamf.org)
A network of university students to help cope with serious illness or deaths of a parent or a loved one. Offers resources and support groups as well as local chapters.

Parents of Murdered Children (PMOC): (www.pomc.org)
A group supporting families who have lost a child or loved one due to homicide. Offers resources and support groups as well as local chapters.

SIDS Alliance: (www.firstcandle.org)
A group supporting parents who have lost a child due to sudden infant death syndrome. Offers resources and support groups as well as local chapters.

Tragedy Assistance Program for Survivors (TAPS): (www.taps.org)
An organization that provides support for families who have lost a person serving in the military. Offers resources and support groups as well as local chapters.

Bereaved Parents of the USA: (www.berereavedparents.org)
A support group for parents who have had a loss. Offers resources and support groups as well as local chapters.

Parents without Partners: (www.parenstwithoutpartners.org)
An organization for single parents and their children that provides education, family activities, and adult social and recreation events. Offers resources and support groups as well as local chapters. Not set up to deal with grief, but with helping you get out there again in society, and supporting you as single parent.

Meetup.com: (www.meetup.com)
The site describes the organization as "Meetups are neighbors getting together to learn something, do something, share something." There are many widow and widower's groups on meet up. You can search geographically for a group near you.

ONLINE GROUPS
(THAT DON'T MEET LIVE, JUST ONLINE)

There are literally millions of grief support groups online—try to find the one that may be right for you.

Facebook: (www.facebook.com) there are several grief groups on Facebook.

Yahoo: (www.yahoo.com) there are over 181,000 grief support groups on Yahoo.

Google: (www.google.com) there are over 250 Google groups about grief.

Linkedin: (www.linkedin.com) there are 116 groups on Linkedin relating to grief.

Griefnet: (www.griefnet.org) support for people grieving.

Online Grief Support: (www.onlinegriefsupport.com) support for people grieving.

Daily Strength: (www.dailystrength.org) support for grieving and many other challenges people face.

Healthfulchat: (www.healthfulchat.org) support for people who are grieving.

Grief Healing: (www.griefhealingdiscussiongroups.com) support for people who are grieving.

Widow Support: (www.widow-support.com) support for widows who are grieving.

GROWW: (www.groww.org) grief recovery online.

National Fallen Firefighters Survivors Support Network: (www.firehero.org) support for people grieving the loss of a fire-fighter killed in the line of duty.

Grief Speaks: (www.griefspeaks.com) support for peo-ple grieving.

Social and Dating Groups

Social Meetup: (www.meetup.com) find other social groups not related to grieving but just getting together with other people.

Moose International: (www.mooseintl.org) a civic, community-based organization for men and women.

Jaycees: (www.jci.cc) a civic, community-based organization for men and women ages 18-40.

Elks: (www.elks.org) a civic, community-based organization for men and women.

Civitans: (www.civitan.com) a civic, community-based organization for men and women.

Dating

eHarmony: (www.eharmony.com) a dating site where people are matched based on core values.

Senior People Meet: (www.seniorpeoplemeet.com) a dating site for people over 50.

Christian Mingle: (www.christianmingle.com) a dating sight for Christians to meet and date other Christians.

Jdate: (www.jdate.com) a dating site for Jewish singles to meet and date other Jewish singles.

Ourtime: (www.ourtime.com) a dating site for people over 50.

It's Just Lunch: (www.itsjustlunch.com) is a service that matches dates and sets them up to have lunch.

BOOKS

Grief and Loss

I Wasn't Ready to Say Goodbye: Coping and Healing After the Sudden Death of a Loved One, Pamela Blair and Noel Brook

Room for Change: Practical Ideas for Reviving after Loss, Susan W. Reynolds

When Bad Things Happen to Good People, Harold Kushner

The Widower's Manual: Unrevealed Cornerstones to Regenerate Your Life, Wouter Looten

On Death and Dying, Elizabeth Kubler-Ross

A Grief Observed, C.S. Lewis

How to Go On Living After Someone You Love Dies, Therese Rando

A New Normal: Learning to Live with Grief and Loss, Darlene Cross

Dream New Dreams: Reimagining My Life After Loss, Jai Pausch

The Grief Recovery Handbook, John James and Russell Freidman

On Grief and Grieving, Elizabeth Kubler-Ross

Broken Open: How Difficult Times Can Help Us Grow, Elizabeth Lesser

The Soul Survivor, Shawn Doyle and Joe Townsend

Coming Apart: Why Relationships End and How to Live Through the Ending of Yours, Daphne Rose Kingma

Motivation

Jumpstart Your Motivation, Shawn Doyle, CSP

Awaken the Giant Within, Anthony Robbins

The Power of Positive Thinking, Norman Vincent Peale

Think and Grow Rich, Napoleon Hill

Do It! Let's Get off Our Buts, John, Rodger, and Peter McWilliams

The Monk Who Sold His Ferrari, Robin Sharma

Man's Search for Meaning, Viktor Frankl

Psycho Cybernetics, Maxwell Maltz

Maximum Achievement, Brian Tracy

The Road Less Traveled, M. Scott Peck

It's Not How Good You Are, It's How Good You Want to Be, Paul Arden

You'll See It When You Believe It, Wayne Dyer

Learned Optimism, Martin Seligman

Acres of Diamonds, Russell Conwell

Attitude Is Everything, Keith Harrell

Masters of Success, Ivan Misner

The 7 Spiritual Laws of Success, Deepak Chopra

The Success System That Never Fails, W. Clement Stone

The 7 Habits of Highly Effective People, Stephen Covey

What Matters Most, Stephen Covey

The Power of Focus, Jack Canfield, Mark Victor Hanson

Stress for Success, Dr. Jim Loehr

Finding Your Voice, Joel Boggess

Two Months to Motivation, Shawn Doyle

MO! Live with Momentum, Motivation, and Moxie, Shawn Doyle and Lauren Anderson

Back from Heaven's Front Porch, Danny Bader

Finance/Money

The Total Money Makeover, Dave Ramsey

The Money Class, Suze Orman

Rich Dad, Poor Dad, Robert Kiyosaki

Communication

The Platinum Rule, Tony Allesandra

I'm OK, You're OK, Thomas Harris

Fierce Conversations, Susan Scott

How to Win Friends and Influence People, Dale Carnegie

Managing Generation Mix, Bruce Tulgan, Carolyn Martin

Creativity

Jumpstart Your Creativity, Shawn Doyle, CSP and Steven Rowell

Jump Start Your Brain, Doug Hall

A Whack in the Side of the Head, Roger Van Oeck

A Kick in the Seat of the Pants, Rodger Van Oeck

Thinkertoys, Michael Milchalko

Jumpstart Your Business Brain, Doug Hall

The Artist Way, Julie Cameron

How to Think Like Leonardo DaVinci, Micheal Gelb

Jamming, John Koa

"There are moments when troubles enter our lives and we can do nothing to avoid them. But they are there for a reason. Only when we have overcome them will we understand why they were there."

—PAULO COELHO, *The Fifth Mountain*

ABOUT SHAWN DOYLE

S HAWN DOYLE, CSP, IS A LEARNING AND DEVELOPMENT professional who has a passion for human potential. He has an avid belief in the concept of lifelong learning. For the last 26 years, Shawn has spent his time developing and implementing training programs on team building, communication, creativity, and leadership. Shawn's training programs help people become more effective in the workplace and in their lives. His clients have included numerous Fortune 500 companies, and his awards and honors are extensive. Shawn is the author of 16 inspirational books.

In this book, he shares the true story of the sudden, tragic death of his wife of 32 years, Cindy. Within this painful loss, Shawn found the means to persevere and create the new life he is living today. He hopes that by applying these ideas and techniques, you will move closer to healing and living again.

OTHER BOOKS BY SHAWN DOYLE

The Soul Survivor (with Captain Joe Townsend)

Jumpstart Your Motivation

Jumpstart Your Leadership

Jumpstart Your Creativity (with Steven Rowell)

Jumpstart Your Customer Service (with Lauren Anderson)

The Manager's Pocket Guide to Motivating Employees

The Manager's Pocket Guide to Training

Dr. Babb's Idea Lab

2 Months to Motivation

6 Essentials for Success (with 5 other authors)

Sales Science (with David Newman)

Juiced! (with David Newman)

Wired! How to be Creative in the World of Cable

Cartoon Magic

The 10 Foundations of Motivation